Model Test Papers

CBSE Class ⑩

For Term 2

MATHEMATICS

Author:
Mr. Mohit Tripathi

<table>
<tr><td>Title</td><td>: Model Test Papers for class -X
Mathematics</td></tr>
<tr><td>Author Name</td><td>: Mr. Mohit Tripathi</td></tr>
<tr><td>Published By</td><td>: EduGorilla Community Pvt. Ltd.</td></tr>
<tr><td>Publishers Address</td><td>: 12/651, First Floor Opp. Arvindo Park, Near Jama Masjid,
Indira Nagar, Lucknow, Uttar Pradesh - 226016, India</td></tr>
</table>

Copyright

Disclaimer

Printed by EduGorilla Community Pvt. Ltd.

SYLLABUS

MATHEMATICS	
Course Structure Class – X (Code No. 041) Latest Syllabus issued by CBSE for Academic Year 2022	
SEMESTER 2 (Marks: 40)	

UNIT NO.	NAME OF THE UNIT
1.	Algebra
2.	Geometry
3.	Trigonometry
4.	Mensuration
5.	Statistics

UNIT 1: ALGEBRA

(i) QUADRATIC EQUATIONS

1. Standard form of a quadratic equation $ax^2 + bx + c = 0$, $(a \neq 0)$. Solutions of quadratic equations (only real roots) by factorization, and by using quadratic formula. Relationship between discriminant and nature of roots.
2. Situational problems based on quadratic equations related to day to day activities to be incorporated.

(ii) ARITHMETIC PROGRESSIONS

Motivation for studying Arithmetic Progression Derivation of the nth term and sum of the first n terms of A.P. and their application in solving daily life problems.

UNIT 2: GEOMETRY

(i) CIRCLES

Tangent to a circle at, point of contact
1. (Prove) The tangent at any point of a circle is perpendicular to the radius through the point of contact.
2. Prove) The lengths of tangents drawn from an external point to a circle are equal.
3. (Motivate) Alternative Segment theorem: If a chord is drawn through the point of contact of a tangent to a circle, then the angles made by the chord with the tangent are respectively equal to the angles subtended by the chord in the alternate segments.

(ii) CONSTRUCTIONS

1. Division of a line segment in a given ratio (internally).
2. Tangents to a circle from a point outside it.
3. Construction of a triangle similar to a given triangle.

UNIT 3: TRIGONOMETRY

(i) HEIGHTS AND DISTANCES

1. Simple problems on heights and distances. Problems should not involve more than two right triangles. Angles of elevation / depression should be only $30°$, $45°$, and $60°$.

UNIT 4: MENSURATION

(i) SURFACE AREAS AND VOLUMES

1. Surface areas and volumes of combinations of any two of the following: cubes, cuboids, spheres, hemispheres and right circular cylinders/cones. Frustum of a cone.
2. Problems involving converting one type of metallic solid into another and other mixed problems. (Problems with combination of not more than two different solids be taken).

UNIT 5: STATISTICS AND PROBABILITY

(i) STATISTICS

1. Mean, median and mode of grouped data (bimodal situation to be avoided). Cumulative frequency graph.

REVISION TECHNIQUE WHY SHOULD YOU REVISE?

You cannot expect to remember all the mathematics concept that you have studied unless revise. It is important to review all your courses, so that you can answer the examination questions.

WHERE SHOULD YOU REVISE?

In a quiet room, with a table and a clock. The room should be brightly lighted. A reading lamp on the table helps you to concentrate on your work and reduces eyestrain.

WHEN SHOULD YOU REVISE?

Being able to focus and revise whenever you feel like it is a great skill but setting a time and regular schedule prepares your brain activity. Start your revision early morning or early each evening before your brain gets tired.

HOW SHOULD YOU REVISE?

If you sit down to revise without thinking of a definite finishing time, you will find that your learning efficiency falls lower and lower and lower.

If you sit down to revise, saying to yourself that you will stop work after 3 hours, then you're learning efficiency falls at the beginning but rises towards the end as your brain realizes it is coming to the end of the session (see Graph).

We can use this U-shaped curve to help us work more efficiently by splitting a 3-hour session

into 3 shorter sessions, each of about 50 minutes with short, planned breaks between them.

The breaks must be planned so that the graph rises near the end of each short session how much you gain:

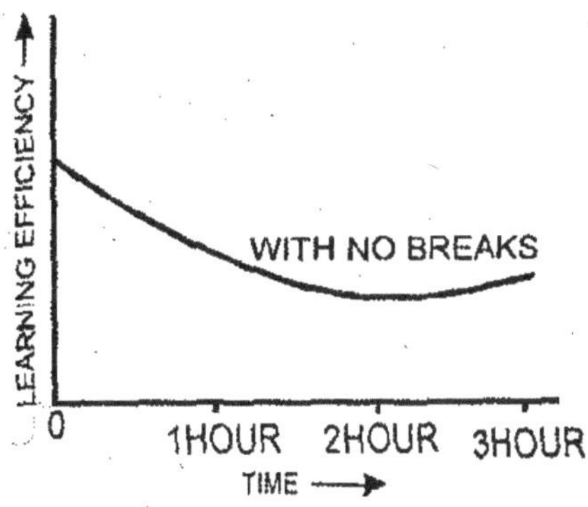

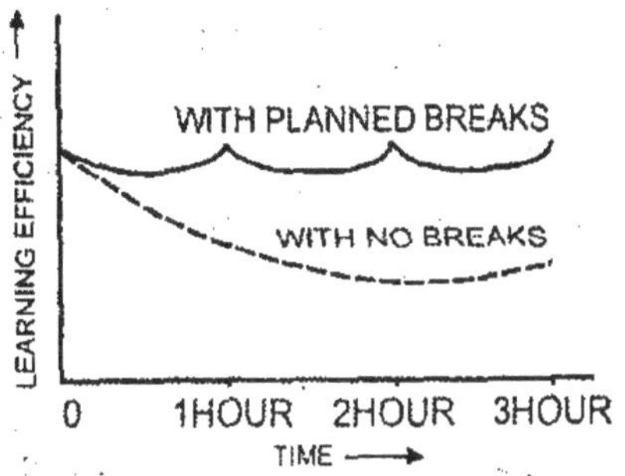

For example, if you start your revision at 6.00 p.m. you should look at your clock or watch and say to yourself. I will work until 7.00 p.m. and then stop — neither earlier and nor later'

At 7.00 p.m. you should leave the table for a relaxation break of 10 minutes (or less), returning by 7.10 p.m. when you should say to yourself, I will work until 8.10 p.m. and then stop neither earlier nor later.'

Continuing in this way is more efficient and causes less strain on you. You get through more work, and you feel less tired.

HOW OFTEN SHOULD YOU REVISE?

The adjoining graphs show the amount of information that your memory can recall at different times after you have finished a revision session the graph rises at the beginning. This is because your brain is still sorting out the information that you have been learning

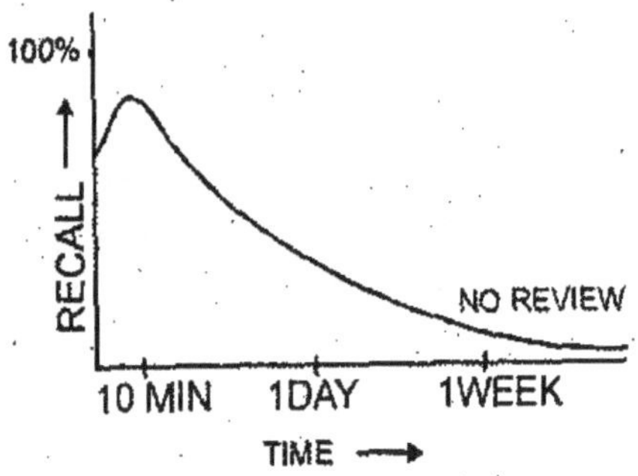

The graph soon falls rapidly so that after 1 day you may remember only about a quarter of what you had learned.

There are two ways of improving your recall process and raising this graph

If you briefly revise the same work again after 10 minutes (at the high point of the graph) then the graph falls much more slowly.

This fits in with your 10-minute break between revision sessions.

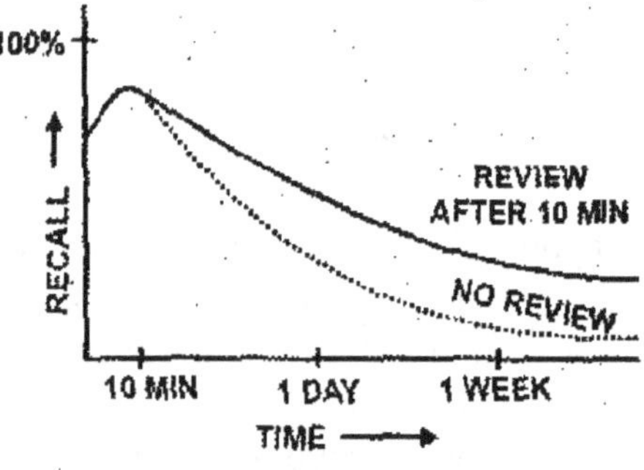

Using the example on the last page, when you return to your table at 7.10 p.m. the first thing you should do is review, the work you learned before 7.00 pm

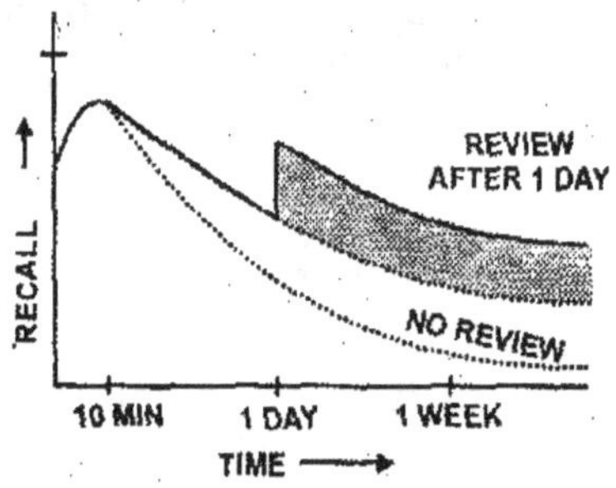

The graph can be lifted again by briefly reviewing the work after 1 day and then again after 1 week. That is, on Tuesday night you should look through the work you learned on Monday night and the work you learned on the previous Tuesday night so that it is fixed equate firmly in your long-term memory.

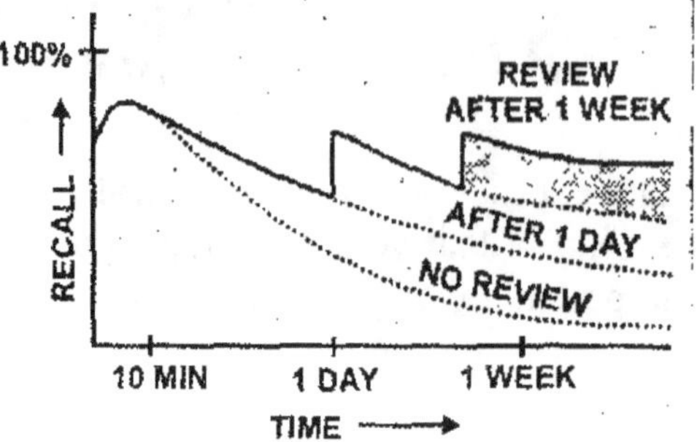

Another method of improving your memory is by taking care to try to understand all parts of your work. This makes all the graphs rise higher.

If you learn your work in a parrot fashion (as you have to do with telephone numbers), all these graphs will be lower. On the occasions when you have to learn facts by heart, try to picture them as exaggerated, colourful images in our mind

REMEMBER

The most important points about revision are that it must occur often and be repeated at the right intervals.

TIPS FOR YOUR BOARD EXAMINATION.

The moment Board Examinations stealthily approach the lives of students, many of them start panicking about the huge syllabus, preparation, revision and the result thereof Students start getting nervous just before the exams and start searching for ways to release their paranoia. To release Then with such stress and tension please follow some steps given below for **10th Board Examination** Preparation.

1. The first step for every student should be to get a thorough knowledge of the latest syllabus by referring to the **CBSE COUNCIL** for **TERM – 2**. After that, they should make a timetable for themselves which would provide them with a schedule, that would help them plan their syllabus and concentrate better.

2. The one thing that students should note before sitting down to study is to make sure that the place in which they are going to study is free from gadgets like computers, TV, radio, mobile, etc. Another thing that equally needs to be avoided is

talking with friends while studying; they can do so when they are finished with studying or when they are free.

3. Students are also provided with previous year sample papers by many publications which can be of great help as they can be solved on an everyday basis. They help in analyzing the mistakes that are being committed and that can be worked upon. By having the latest papers students get an idea of the type of questions expected, and the level of difficulty in the Board Exam.

4. In order to score high marks students, tend to revert to the use of malpractices. In many cases, they cram down the syllabus, instead of trying to understand it. They need to understand that both of these methods are wrong in the present and for the future. Cramming without understanding, will take them nowhere, and using wrong means can lead to them being caught and not being able to attempt the paper.

5. In order to feel fresh and energetic the whole day, students should always **eat and sleep well**. They should always have an early dinner and should not study till late night (specially a night before the exam). Fast food and greasy food should be avoided as much as possible and a habit of getting up early to study should be adopted.

6. Making notes and practicing all the problems by **writing them down** rather than verbally learn in them is one of the best tricks to remember and understand the course. Students can also make brief notes of every chapter so that they can refer to them without needing to open their textbook every time.

7. Taking help when in doubt or in any kind of problem should be done by the students well on time. Doubts can be cleared by meeting the concerned teachers, friends, and seniors.

8. The idea of not taking breaks in between and studying continually is a mistake often committed by students.

9. Students should avoid mood swings and personal problems that may prevent them from studying and completing their work. They should always try and remain in a jolly and happy mood and ignore the problems that come in their way. This will help them concentrate better.

10. Students should always learn and practice **time management**. They should work on their writing speed so that they can write fast and neat and not miss any questions while attempting the paper.

11. Don't neglect your health. Just because you're short of time doesn't mean you should live on junk foodie Try to get your **fruits** and **vegetables** every day. Remember to **exercise (breathing yoga)** at least 30 minutes a day. Doing these things will support mental, physical, and emotional function:

12. It's not a good idea to pick up your books and start working until you're finished— because you may not have enough time to accomplish all your tasks. Figure out how much time you have for each assignment, and plot this out in your calendar. Try to give yourself some extra time for each assignment in case one takes longer than you expected. When you plot out your time, be sure to schedule study breaks. Working straight through without a break can make you less efficient and somewhat insane.

13. Set a time limit on how long you study for each class. Don't go overboard on one subject and forget that you have several others to catch up on before going to bed. Also, don't rush through studying; take your time and **concentrate**. You may want to set an alarm clock at a certain hour, so when it rings, go to another subject, and reset the alarm.

14. Get at least **6 hours of sleep**. If you have more or less sleep than you should have, you may start lacking in your coursework and become lazy because of the urge or want to sleep.

Tips for Mathematics (which leads to marks deduction):

Don't forget to write a formula before calculation
Write complete solution (don't skip steps). In some problems like equations with variables, one can check the solution(s) by substituting them back in the equation(s).
In graphs, plot them neatly.
Don't forget to write units (if any).

Show complete working, avoid to solve questions in a rough sheet, and write only answers.

Try to write solutions in an aligned manner. Write formulas/theorems or concepts on paper and stick-on walls so that they make an image in your mind.

May the force be with you.

CBSE X MATHEMATICS

UNIT - 1

ALGEBRA

CHAPTER

Quadratic Equations

1.1 Introduction: A Polynomial is a mathematical expression of one or more algebraic terms. Polynomial expressions include constant, variables and exponent of variables, where exponent of variables must be non negative integer (**whole** number).

For Example: $3, x + 1, x^2 + 5x + 6$ etc. are polynomials of degree 0, degree 1, and degree 2 respectively.

Degree of a polynomial is the highest power of variable of any term.

1.2 Quadratic polynomial: Degree 2 polynomials are called quadratic polynomials. When we equate this polynomial to zero, we get a **Quadratic Equation**.

For example: $x^2 + 5x + 6 = 0$

1.3 Standard form of a quadratic equation: A quadratic equation in variable x of the form $ax^2 + bx + c = 0$, where $a \neq 0$ is called **standard** form of a quadratic equation. Here $a, b,$ and c are real numbers. For example, $3x^2 + 5x - 6$ is a quadratic equation. Here $a = 3, b = 5$ and $c = -6$.

$-2x + x^2 + 2 = 0, 6 - 5x + x^2 = 0$ are also few examples of quadratic equations. But try to write any quadratic equation in descending order of their degrees.

1.4 Roots/zeroes/solutions of a quadratic equation: Let $x^2 - 5x + 6 = 0$ is a quadratic equation. Put $x = 2$ and 3 one by one, what happened? The left hand side of the equation equals to the right hand side. Can any other value equate this equation to 0? No. So, these two values are called **zeroes/roots/solutions** of the quadratic equation.

Root is that real value of the variable used in quadratic equation, which satisfies the quadratic equation. So, if $x = \beta$ is a root of $ax^2 + bx + c = 0, a \neq 0$, then $a\beta^2 + b\beta + c = 0$. In other words value of x which equates any quadratic equation to 0 is called **root**. A quadratic equation has **exactly two real roots (if exist).** Otherwise, imaginary roots (out of syllabus)

In this chapter, we will try to find these two real roots (where possible).

There are **three algebraic** and a **graphical** method to find these roots. Three algebraic methods are:

- Factorization (Split the middle term)
- Quadratic formula
- Completing the square method (Not in syllabus)

1.5: Discriminant: Before start solving any quadratic equation, let's discuss a very **important** term of a quadratic equation, behavior of a quadratic equation depends on it. For a quadratic equation $ax^2 + bx + c = 0, a \neq 0$,

$$\text{discriminant } (d) = b^2 - 4ac$$

Roots (real) are possible only if $b^2 - 4ac \geq 0$.

1.6 Solution of a quadratic equation using factorization method: We can find roots of a quadratic equation using factorization method if discriminant (d) = $b^2 - 4ac$ is a **perfect square.**
For example for $2x^2 - 5x - 3 = 0$ discriminant $(d) = (-5)^2 - 4 \times 2 \times (-3) \Rightarrow 25 + 24 \Rightarrow 49$ (which is a perfect square as $7 \times 7 = 49$).

Method: let $ax^2 + bx + c = 0, a \neq 0$, is a quadratic equation.
Step 1: First find $a \times c$ (with sign).
Step 2: Find two factors (let p and q) satisfying $p \times q = a \times c$ so that $p \pm q = b$.
Step 3: With these values of p and q, factorize the given quadratic equation.
For example: Solve the quadratic $2x^2 - 5x - 3 = 0$ using factorization method.
Solution:
Here $a = 2, b = -5, c = -3$, so $a \times c = 2 \times (-3) = -6$
Now $-6 \times 1 = -6$ and $-6 + 1 = -5$, so required factors are -6 and 1.
So, $2x^2 - 5x - 3 = 0$

$$2x^2 - 6x + 1x - 3 = 0$$
$$2x(x - 3) + 1(x - 3) = 0$$
$$(2x + 1)(x - 3) = 0$$
$$2x + 1 = 0, \text{ or } x - 3 = 0 \text{ (Apply zero product rule)}$$
$$x = -\frac{1}{2}, \text{ or } x = 3. \text{ Ans.}$$

1.7 Solution of a quadratic equation using quadratic formula: Sometimes it is not possible to solve a quadratic equation using factorization method (as $b^2 - 4ac$ is not a perfect square), then **quadratic formula** is used to solve the quadratic equation.
If $ax^2 + bx + c = 0, a \neq 0$, is a quadratic equation then the roots are given by:

$$x = \frac{-b \pm \sqrt{b^2 - 4ac}}{2a}.$$

Proving of quadratic formula:
Consider the quadratic equation $ax^2 + bx + c = 0, a \neq 0$
Multiplying both side by $4a$ we get: $4a^2x^2 + 4abx + 4ac = 0$

$$4a^2x^2 + 4abx = -4ac$$
$$4a^2x^2 + 4abx + b^2 = -4ac + b^2 (\text{add } b^2 \text{ both sides to make LHS a perfect square })$$
$$(2ax)^2 + 2 \times (2ax) \times b + b^2 = -4ac + b^2$$
$$(2ax + b)^2 = b^2 - 4ac$$
$$2ax + b = \pm\sqrt{b^2 - 4ac} \qquad [a^2 + 2 \times a \times b + (b)^2 = (a + b)^2]$$
$$2ax = -b \pm \sqrt{b^2 - 4ac}$$
$$x = \frac{-b \pm \sqrt{b^2 - 4ac}}{2a}$$

1.8 Nature of roots: A quadratic equation has two roots which may be real or imaginary, rational or irrational, equal or distinct. The nature of roots depends on the value of **discriminant $b^2 - 4ac.$**
If $ax^2 + bx + c = 0$, where a, b and c are real numbers and, $a \neq 0$, then
- If $b^2 - 4ac = 0 \rightarrow$ then Roots are **Real** and **Equal.**
  For example: $x^2 + 4x + 4 = 0$
- If $b^2 - 4ac > 0(+ve) \rightarrow$ then Roots are **Real** and **Distinct.**
  For example: $x^2 + 5x - 6 = 0$

- If $b^2 - 4ac < 0(-ve) \rightarrow$ then Roots are **Imaginary (not real)**.
  For example: $x^2 + 2x + 5 = 0$

Practice Sheet - 1

1. Short questions (for one or two marks):

(i) Find the value of x, if $a + 1 = 0$ and $x^2 + ax - 6 = 0$.

(ii) Determine whether $x = -1$ is a root of the equation $x^2 - 3x + 2 = 0$.

(iii) If $x = \dfrac{2}{3}$ is a solution of the quadratic equation $7x^2 + mx - 3 = 0$; find the value of m

(iv) If quadratic equation $x^2 - (m + 1)x + 6 = 0$ has one root as $x = 3$; find the value of m and the other root of the equation.

(v) If $\dfrac{1}{2}$ is a root of the equation $x^2 + kx - \dfrac{5}{4} = 0$, find the value of k.

(vi) The value(s) of p for which the quadratic equation $2x^2 + 3x + p = 0$ has no real roots is:

    (a) $p > \dfrac{9}{8}$ (b) $p < \dfrac{9}{8}$ (c) $p = \dfrac{9}{8}$ (d) $p \neq \dfrac{9}{8}$

(vii) If the equation $x^2 - 4x + k = 0$ has equal roots, then find the value of 'k'.

(viii) If the discriminant of the equation $6x^2 - bx + 2 = 0$ is 1, then the value of b:

    (a) 7   (b) -7 (c) ± 7 (d) $\pm\sqrt{7}$

(ix) If the roots of $ax^2 + bx + c = 0$ are equal in magnitude but opposite in sign, Then:

    (a) $a = 0$ (b) $b = 0$ (c) $c = 0$ (d) $b^2 = 4ac$

(x) If $ax^2 + bx + c = 0$ has equal roots, then c is:

    (a) $\dfrac{b}{2a}$ (b) $\dfrac{-b}{2a}$ (c) $\dfrac{b^2}{4a}$ (d) $\dfrac{-b^2}{4a}$

2. Solve using factorization method:

(i) $3x^2 - 14x + 8 = 0$

(ii) $2x^2 - 8x - 24 = 0$

(iii) $\sqrt{3}x^2 + 10x + 7\sqrt{3} = 0$

(iv) $21x^2 - 2x + \dfrac{1}{21} = 0$

(v) $\sqrt{7}x^2 - 6x - 13\sqrt{7} = 0$

(vi) $\dfrac{x+3}{x+2} = \dfrac{3x-7}{2x-3}$

(vii) $x^2 - 2bx + (b^2 - a^2) = 0$

(viii) $12abx^2 - (9a^2 - 8b^2)x - 6ab = 0$

(ix) $x^2 + 4x - (a^2 + 2a - 3) = 0$

(x) $9^{x+2} - 6 \times 3^{x+1} + 1 = 0$

(xi) $5^{x+1} + 5^{2-x} = 5^3 + 1$

3. Find the roots of the following equations, if they exist, using the Quadratic Formula:

(i) $2x^2 - 5x + 3 = 0$

(ii) $x^2 + 4x + 5 = 0$

(iii) $\sqrt{3}x^2 + 2\sqrt{2}x - 2\sqrt{3} = 0$

(iv) $\dfrac{x^2}{2} - \sqrt{11}x + 1 = 0$

(v) $\dfrac{1}{x+1} + \dfrac{2}{x+2} - \dfrac{4}{x+4} = 0; x \neq -1, -2, -4$

(vi) $36x^2 - 12ax + (a^2 - b^2) = 0$

(vii) $12abx^2 - (9a^2 - 8b^2)x - 6ab = 0$

4. Comment on the nature of the roots of the quadratic equation $4x^2 - 5 = 2(x + 1)^2 - 7$

5. Comment on the nature of the roots of the quadratic equation $12abx^2 - (9a^2 - 8b^2)x - 6ab = 0$

6. Find the value of k for which the roots of the following equations are real and equal:

(i) $8kx(x - 1) + 1 = 0$

(ii) $x^2 + 2(k - 1)x + (k + 5) = 0$

(iii) $x^2 - 8kx + 2k = 0$

(iv) $(k - 12)x^2 + 2(k - 12)x + 2 = 0$

7. If the equation $(1 + m^2)x^2 + 2mcx + (c^2 - a^2) = 0$ has equal roots of x, prove that: $c^2 = a^2(1 + m^2)$.

8. If roots of a quadratic equation $(b - c)x^2 + (c - a)x + (a - b) = 0$ are real and equal, then prove that $2b = a + c$.

9. The roots of the quadratic equation $(a^2 + b^2)x^2 - 2(ac + bd)x + (c^2 + d^2) = 0$ are equal. Prove that $\dfrac{a}{b} = \dfrac{c}{d}$

ANSWERS

Short questions (for one or two marks)		
Answer 1.	(i)	$[3, -2]$
	(ii)	no
	(iii)	$\left[-\dfrac{1}{6}\right]$
	(iv)	$m = 4, x = 2$
	(v)	2
	(vi)	a
	(vii)	4
	(viii)	c
	(ix)	b
	(x)	c
Solve using factorization method		
Answer 2.	(i)	$4, \dfrac{2}{3}$
	(ii)	$6, -2$
	(iii)	$-\sqrt{3}, -\dfrac{7\sqrt{3}}{3}$
	(iv)	$\dfrac{1}{21}, \dfrac{1}{21}$
	(v)	$13/\sqrt{7}, -\sqrt{7}$
	(vi)	$5, -1$

	(vii)	$(b-a), (b+a)$
	(viii)	$\dfrac{3a}{4b}, \dfrac{-2b}{3a}$
	(ix)	$-(a+3), (a-1)$
	(x)	$-2, -2$
	(xi)	$2, -1$
Answer 3.	**(i)**	$\dfrac{3}{2}, 1$
	(ii)	No real roots
	(iii)	$\dfrac{\sqrt{6}}{3}, -\sqrt{6}$
	(iv)	$(\sqrt{11}+3), (\sqrt{11}-3)$
	(v)	$2+2\sqrt{3},\ 2-2\sqrt{3}$
	(vi)	$\dfrac{a+b}{6}, \dfrac{a-b}{6},$
	(vii)	$\dfrac{3a}{4b}, \dfrac{-2b}{3a}$
Answer 4.		Real and unequal
Answer 5.		Real and unequal
Answer 6.	**(i)**	$k = \dfrac{1}{2}$
	(ii)	$4, -1$
	(iii)	$0, \dfrac{1}{8}$
	(iv)	14

Problem sums: There are so many types of problem sums. For example, age, two digits number, two numbers, fraction, consecutive numbers, consecutive even/odd numbers, work and time, area and perimeter, right angled triangle, upstream and downstream, speed and time, profit and loss, and many more. To solve a problem sum, start the question like:

- Let the unknown quantity, which is asked in the question $= x$

- Try to represent the given problem in the form of quadratic equation.

- Solve the equation.

Practice Sheet - 2

(Based on word problems)

1. The product of two numbers is 192. If they are differ by 4. Find the numbers.

2. The sum of two numbers is 15. If the sum of their reciprocals is $\dfrac{3}{10}$. Find the numbers.

3. Three consecutive natural numbers are such that the square of the middle number exceeds the difference of the squares of the other two by 60. Find the numbers.

4. A two digit number is such that the product of its digits is 18. When 63 is subtracted from the number, the digits interchange their places. Find the number.

5. The product of Rahul's age five years ago with his age 9 years later is 15. Find Rahul's present age.

6. Two years ago, a man's age was three times the square of his son's age. In three years' time, his age will be four times his son's age. Find their present ages.

7. The hotel bill for a number of people for overnight stay is Rs. 4,800 If there were 4 people more, the bill each person had to pay would have reduced by Rs. 200 Find the number of people staying overnight.

8. A shopkeeper purchases a certain number of books for Rs. 960. If the cost per book was Rs. 8 less, the number of books that could be purchased for Rs. 960 would be 4 more. Write an equation, taking the original cost of each book to be x, and solve it to find the original cost of the book.

9. In a two digit number, the ten's digit is bigger. The product of the digits is 27 and the difference between two digits is 6. Find the number.

10. Two pipes are running together can fill a tank in $11\dfrac{1}{9}$ minutes. If one pipe takes 5 minutes more than the other to fill the tank. Find the time in which each pipe would fill the tank.

11. A train travels a distance of 300 km at constant speed. If the speed of the train is increased by 5 km/hour, the journey would have taken two hours less. Find the original speed of train.

12. Perimeter of a rectangular plot is 180 m and its area is 1800 m^2. Find the length and breadth of the plot.

13. A trader bought a number of articles for Rs. 1200. Ten were damaged and he sold each of the rest at Rs. 2 more than what he paid for it, thus clearing a profit of Rs. 60 on the whole transaction. Taking the number of articles he bought as x, form an equation in x and solve it.

14. Five years ago, a woman's age was the square of her son's age. Ten years hence her age will be twice that of her son's age. Find: -

    (i) The age of the son five years ago

    (ii) The present age of the woman.

15. A positive number is divided into two parts such that the sum of the squares of the two parts is 20. The square of the larger part is 8 times the smaller part. Taking x as the smaller part of the two parts, Find the number.

16. A can do a piece of work in 'x' days and B can do the same work in $(x + 16)$ days. If both working together can do it in 15 days; calculate 'x'.

17. The hypotenuse of a right angled triangle exceeds one side by 1 cm and the other side by 18 cm. Find the lengths of the sides of the triangle.

18. An area is paved with square tiles of a certain size and the number required is 128. If the tiles had been 2 cm smaller each way, 200 tiles would have been needed to pave the same area. Find the size of the larger tiles.

19. A man bought an article for Rs. x and sold it for Rs. 16. If his loss was x percent, find the cost price of the article.

20. A motor boat, whose speed is 9 km/hr in still water, goes 12 km downstream and comes back in a total time of 3 hours. Find the speed of the stream.

21. A plane left 30 minutes later than the schedule time and in order to reach its destination 1500 km away in time, it has to increase its speed by 250 km/hr from its usual speed. Find its usual speed.

ANSWERS

Answer 1.	$-12, -16$ or $12, 16$
Answer 2.	10, 5
Answer 3.	9, 10, 11
Answer 4.	92
Answer 5.	6 years
Answer 6.	29 years, 5 years
Answer 7.	8
Answer 8.	Rs. 48
Answer 9.	93
Answer 10.	20 minutes and 25 minutes
Answer 11.	25 Km/hr
Answer 12.	60 m, 30 m
Answer 13.	100
Answer 14.	5yrs, 30yrs
Answer 15.	6
Answer 16.	24
Answer 17.	25 cm, 24 cm, 7 cm
Answer 18.	10 cm
Answer 19.	Rs. 20 or Rs. 80
Answer 20.	3 km/hr
Answer 21.	750 km/hr

1.1 Introduction: A sequence is a collection of something in such a way that it has an identified first, second, third member and so on. Every member in it is called a **term**. It is not necessary that the every sequence has a certain pattern like amount of money deposited in bank. Those sequences whose terms flows a certain pattern or rule are called **Progression. For example,**

1, 2, 4, 8, 16, and so on.

1, 4, 7, 10, 13, and so on.

1.2 Arithmetic Progression: A sequence . $a_1, a_2, a_3, \ldots \ldots a_n$ is called an **Arithmetic progression** or sequence, if there exists a **constant d** (which can be positive or negative or zero) such that:

$a_2 - a_1 = a_3 - a_2 = a_4 - a_3 = d$ and so on. Here d is the common difference, (i.e, d = any term – its previous term)

So common difference $(d) = a_{n+1} - a_n$

Some **examples** of arithmetic progressions (with common differences) are as follows:

$1, 3, 5, 7, \ldots \ldots, and\ so\ on\ (d = 3 - 1 = 2)$

$1, 2.5, 4, 5.5, \ldots \ldots, and\ so\ on\ (d = 2.5 - 1 = 1.5)$

$5, 1, -3, -7, \ldots \ldots, and\ so\ on\ (d = 1 - 5 = -4)$

$\sqrt{2}, 2\sqrt{2}, 3\sqrt{3}, \ldots \ldots,$ and so on $(d = 2\sqrt{2} - \sqrt{2} = \sqrt{2})$

$\sqrt{3}, \sqrt{12}, \sqrt{27}, \sqrt{48}, \ldots \ldots$ is equivalent to $\sqrt{3}, 2\sqrt{3}, 3\sqrt{3}, 4\sqrt{3}, \ldots \ldots (d = 2\sqrt{3} - \sqrt{3} = \sqrt{3})$

1.3 Standard/general form of an Arithmetic Progression: Let 'a' be the first term of an A.P. and 'd' be the common difference, the terms of an A.P. $a_1, a_2, a_3, \ldots$, and so on can be taken as:

$a_1 = a$

$a_2 = a + d$

$a_3 = a + 2d,$

Following this pattern, **general term** or **nth term** is given by:

$$a_n = a + (n - 1)d$$

From the above formula of **nth** term we can write any term in standard form, like 10 term: $a_{10} = a + 9d.$

$$a_1 \quad a_2 \quad a_3 \quad a_4 \qquad\qquad a_n$$

$$a, (a + d), (a + 2d), (a + 3d), \ldots \ldots, [a + (n - 1)d]$$

Remark: If an A.P. has only n terms, then its nth term will be the **last term** is denoted by $l = a + (n - 1)d.$

1.4 rth term from the end of an A.P: If an A.P. has n terms, then rth term from the end = n – (r – 1)th term from the beginning.

For example: To find 10 terms from the end of an A.P. of 30 terms. Find its $30 - (10 - 1) = 21$st term from the beginning of the original A.P.

1.5 Arithmetic mean: If 'a', 'A' and 'b' are in A.P., then 'A' is called **Arithmetic mean** between 'a' and 'b'. Since 'a', 'A' and 'b' are is A.P., so their common difference will be equal

And, $=> A - a = b - A => A = \dfrac{a+b}{2}$

So Arithmetic mean between 'a' and 'b' $= \dfrac{a+b}{2}$

Remark: To an A.P. if we add, subtract, multiply or divide each term by the same number (in case of division, the number should be non-zero), the resulting sequence would always be an A.P.

Practice Sheet - 1

(Based on n^{th} term)

1. Short questions (for one or two marks):

(i) If $p - 1, p + 3, 3p - 1$ are in A.P., then p is equal to:

    (a) 4   (b) -4 (c) 2   (d) -2

(ii) If $21, a, b, -3$ are in A.P. Find the value of $a + b$.

(iii) 15th term of the A.P. $x - 7, x - 2, x + 3, \ldots$ is:

    (a) $x + 63$ (b) $x + 73$ (c) $x + 83$ (d) $x + 53$

(iv) The common difference of an A.P. in which $a_{25} - a_{12} = -52$ is:

    (a) 4   (b) -4   (c) -3   (d) 3

(v) Find the number of the terms in the following series: $-5 + (-8) + (-11) + \ldots + (-230)$

(vi) $37th$ term of the A.P.: $\sqrt{x}, 3\sqrt{x}, 5\sqrt{x}, \ldots \ldots$ is:

    (a) $37\sqrt{x}$ (b) $39\sqrt{x}$ (c) $73\sqrt{x}$ (d) $75\sqrt{x}$

(vii) If $(k - 3), (2k + 1)$, and $(4k + 3)$ are three consecutive terms of an A.P. Find the value of k.

(viii) How many numbers of two digits are divisible by 7 ?

(ix) Is 184 a term of the sequence $3, 7, 11, \ldots \ldots$?

(x) Which term of the sequence $-1, 3, 7, 11, \ldots$ is 95?

(xi) How many terms are there in the sequence $3, 6, 9, 12, \ldots 111$?

(xii) Find the common difference and write the next three terms of the A.P. $3, -2, -7, -12, \ldots$

2. Three marks questions:

(i) Show that the sequence defined by $a_n = 4n + 5$ is an A.P. Also find its common difference.

(ii) Show that the sequence defined by $a_n = 2n^2 + 1$ is not an A.P.

(iii) The nth term of a sequence is $3n - 2$. Is the sequence an A.P. ? If so, find its $10th$ term?

(iv) Find the $12th, 24th$ and nth term of the A.P. given by $9, 13, 17, 21, 25, \ldots \ldots$

(v) Show that the sequence $9, 12, 15, 18, \ldots$ is an A.P. Find its $16th$ term and the general term.

(vi) The first term of an A.P. is -7 and the common difference is 5. Find its $18th$ term and the general term.

(vii) Which term of the sequence $20, 19, 18, 17, \ldots$ is the first negative term?

(viii) The $10th$ term of an A.P. is 52 and $16th$ term is 82. Find the $32nd$ term and the general term.

(ix) Determine the general term of an A.P. whose $7th$ term is -1 and $16th$ term 17.

(x) If five times the fifth term of an A.P. is equal to 8 times its eighth term, show that its $13th$ term is zero.

(xi) Find the number of integers between 50 and 500 which are divisible by 7.

(xii) Which term of the A.P. 3,15,27,39,....... will be 132 more than its $54th$ term?

(xiii) In an arithmetic progression the fourth and the sixth terms are 8 and 14 respectively. Find:
(i) first term (ii) common difference

(xiv) Find the $10th$ term from the end of the A.P. 4, 9, 14, ..., 254.

(xv) Determine 'a' so that $2a + 1, a^2 + a + 1$ and $3a^2 - 3a + 3$ are consecutive terms of an A.P.

3. Four marks questions:

(i) For what value of n, the nth terms of the A.P. 63, 65, 67, . . . and 3, 10, 17, . . . are equal? Also, find that term.

(ii) In an A.P., prove that $a_{m+n} + a_{m-n} = 2a_m$, where a_n denotes nth term of the A.P.

(iii) A manufacturer of T.V. sets produced 600 sets in the third year and 700 sets in the seventh year. Assuming that the production increases uniformly by a fixed number every year, find:
(i) The production in the first year.
(ii) The production in the 10th year.

(iv) The third term of an A.P. is 7 and the seventh term exceeds three times the third term by 2. Find the first term and the common difference.

(v) If m times the mth term of an A.P. is the same as n times its nth term, find the $(m + n)^{th}$ term.

(vi) In the sequence 2, 5, 8, . . . up to 50 terms and 3, 5, 7, . . . up to 60 terms, find the number of identical terms.

$$\boxed{\textbf{ANSWERS}}$$

Short questions (for one or two marks)		
Answer 1.	(i)	a
	(ii)	18
	(iii)	a
	(iv)	b
	(v)	76
	(vi)	c
	(vii)	$k = 2$
	(viii)	13
	(ix)	No
	(x)	25
	(xi)	37
	(xii)	$-5; -17, -22, -27$
Three marks questions		
Answer 2.	(i)	4
	(iii)	Yes, 28
	(iv)	53, 101, 4n +5
	(v)	54, 3n + 6
	(vi)	78, 5n -12
	(vii)	28th
	(viii)	162; 5n + 2
	(ix)	2n – 15
	(xi)	64
	(xii)	65th
	(xiii)	$-1, 3$
	(xiv)	209
	(xv)	1, 2
Four marks questions		
Answer 3.	(i)	n = 13, term = 27
	(iii)	(i) 550 (ii) 775
	(iv)	$-1, 4$
	(v)	0
	(vi)	20

1.6 Sum of n terms of an A.P.: Now we will calculate the sum of the Arithmetic progression. Let for a given A.P. first term = a, common difference = d and last term = l, so sum of n terms of the following A.P. is given by:

(i) a, n and l are known then $S_n = \dfrac{n}{2}(a + l)$

(ii) a, n and d are known then $S_n = \dfrac{n}{2}[2a + (n - 1)d]$

Proving of the following formulas:

Let 'a' be the first term, 'd' be the common difference and 'l' be the last term then sum of terms of the A.P. is given by:

$\Rightarrow S = a + (a + d) + (a + 2d) + \ldots\ldots\ldots\ldots + (l - 2d) + (l - d) + l$ (i)

Now writing the terms of the A.P. in reverse order:

$\Rightarrow S = l + (l - d) + (l - 2d) + \ldots\ldots\ldots\ldots\ldots + (a + 2d) + (a + d) + a$ (ii)

Now adding equation (i) and (ii) we get:

$\Rightarrow 2S = (a + l) + (a + d + l - d) + (a + 2d + l - 2d) + \ldots\ldots\ldots + (l - 2d + a + 2d) + (l - d + a + d) + (l + a)$

$\Rightarrow 2S = (a + l) + (a + l) + (a + l)\ldots\ldots\ldots\ $ n times

$\Rightarrow 2S = n(a + l)$

$\Rightarrow S = \dfrac{n}{2}(a + l)$

Since, $l = a + (n - 1)d$, so put this value in the derived formula

$\Rightarrow S = \dfrac{n}{2}[2a + (n - 1)d]$

1.7 Formula of nth term using the formula of the sum of n terms of an A.P.:

$$a_n = S_n - S_{n-1}$$

For example: $a_5 = S_5 - S_4$

1.8 Special cases (Sum of there or more terms in A.P.):

- When sum of Three consecutive terms in A.P. is given then take terms as **(a – d), a, and (a + d)**.

- When sum of four consecutive terms in A.P. is given then take terms as **(a – 3d), (a – d), (a + d), and (a + 3d)**.

- When sum of five consecutive terms in A.P. is given then take terms as **(a – 2d), (a – d), a, (a + d), and (a + 2d)**.

Practice Sheet - 2

(Based on sum of n terms)

1. Short questions (for one or two marks):

(i) The sum of all natural numbers from 1 to 100:

    (a) 4050   (b) 5050   (c) 6050   (d) 7050

(ii) The sum of the first n terms of an A.P. is $2n^2 + 5n$. Then its nth term is:

    (a) 4n + 3   (b) 4n – 3   (c) 3n – 4   (d) 3n + 4

(iii) If an A.P. has a = 1, t_n = 20 and S_n = 399, then value of n is:

    (a) 20   (b) 32   (c) 38   (d) 40

(iv) The sum of first 10 multiples of 2:
   (a) 100   (b) 110   (c) 130   (d) 120

(v) Sum of first n terms of the series $\sqrt{2} + \sqrt{8} + \sqrt{18} + \ldots$ is:
   (a) $\dfrac{n(n+1)}{2}$ (b) $\sqrt{2}n$ (c) $\dfrac{n(n+1)}{\sqrt{2}}$ (d) 1

(vi) The nth term of an A.P. is $T_n = 2n + 1$. Find its sum.

(vii) If the nth term of a sequence is given by $t_n = 3 - 4n$. Find the sum of the first sixteen terms of the sequence.

2. Three marks questions:

(i) The sum of first, third and seventeenth terms of an A.P. is 216. Find the sum of the first 13 terms of the A.P.

(ii) If the sum of all the terms of an A.P. 1, 4, 7, 10, ..., m is 287 find *m*.

(iii) If the angles of a triangle are in A.P. the greatest angle is twice the least. Find all angles of the triangle.

(iv) Find the sum of all three digit numbers which leave the remainder 2 when divided by 3.

(v) The sum of first q terms of an A.P. is $63q - 3q^2$. If its pth term is –60. Find the value of p. Also, find the 11th term of this A.P.

(vi) In an A.P., 6th term is half the 4th term, and the 3rd term is 15. How many terms are needed to give a sum that is equal to 66?

3. Four marks questions:

(i) If the sum of three numbers in A.P. is 21 and their product is 231, find the numbers.

(ii) In an A.P. the sum of first 10 terms is –80 and the sum of next ten terms is –280. Find the A.P.

(iii) If the sum of first m terms of an A.P. is n and the sum of first n terms is m, then show that the sum of its first $(m + n)$ terms is $-(m + n)$.

(iv) Jaipal Singh repays the total loan of Rs. 118,000 by paying every month starting with the first installment of Rs. 1000. If he increases the installment by Rs. 100 every month, what amount will be paid by him in the $30th$ installment? What amount of loan does he still have to pay after $30th$ installment?

(v) If the pth term of an A.P. is $\dfrac{1}{q}$ and the qth term is $\dfrac{1}{p}$, show that the sum of first pq terms is $\dfrac{(pq+1)}{2}$.

(vi) The sum of first m terms of an A.P. is $4m^2 - m$. If its nth term is 107, find the value of n. Also, find the 21st term of this A.P.

(vii) 360 bricks are stacked in the following manner: 30 bricks in the bottom row, 29 in the next row, 28 in the row next to it and so on. In how many rows are the 360 bricks placed and how many bricks are there in the top row?

(viii) Divide 32 into four parts which are in A.P. such that the product of extremes is to the product of means is 7 : 15.

ANSWERS

Short questions (for one or two mark)		
Answer 1.	**(i)**	b
	(ii)	a
	(iii)	c
	(iv)	b
	(v)	c
	(vi)	$n^2 + 2n$
	(vii)	-496
Three marks questions		
Answer 2.	**(i)**	936
	(ii)	40
	(iii)	$40^\circ, 60^\circ, 80^\circ$
	(iv)	164850
	(v)	21, 0
	(vi)	4 or 11
Four marks questions		
Answer 3.	**(i)**	3, 7, 11 or 11, 7, 3
	(ii)	1, -1, -3
	(iv)	Rs. 3900, Rs. 44500
	(vi)	14, 163
	(vii)	16 rows, 15 bricks
	(viii)	2, 6, 10, 14

1.1 Introduction: Set of all points in a plane which are at a constant distance from a fixed point is called a circle. Or the locus (path) traced out by a moving point, at a fixed distance from a fixed point in the same plane.

- The fixed point is called the **center** of the circle and the constant distance is called **radius** of the circle.
- The outer boundary or perimeter of the circle is called **circumference**.
- A line which intersects the circle at two distinct point is called **secant**.
- A line segment, which touches the circle at two distinct points is called **chord**.
- A chord which passes through center is called **diameter**. It is the **longest** chord of the circle. Its length is double of the **radius**. Diameter = 2×radius.

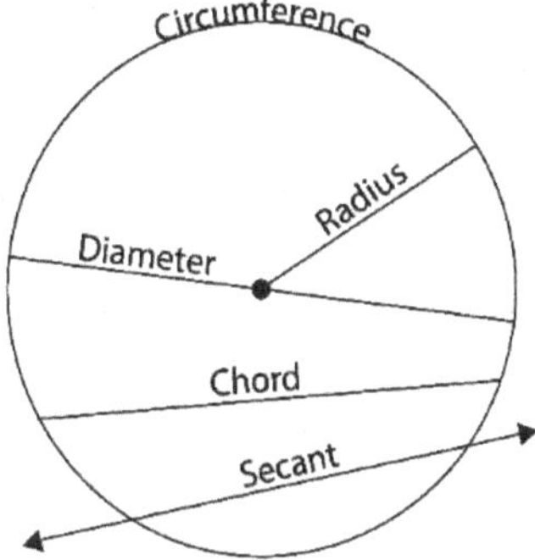

1.2 Circumscribed circle: If a circle contains a polygon inside itself so that all vertices of the polygon touches boundary of the circle, called **circumscribed circle**. The center of circumscribed circle is called **circumcentre** and the polygon is called **inscribed polygon**. The following figures are examples of circumscribed circle.

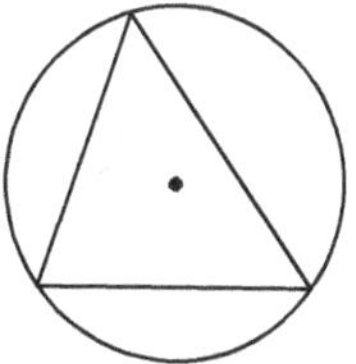 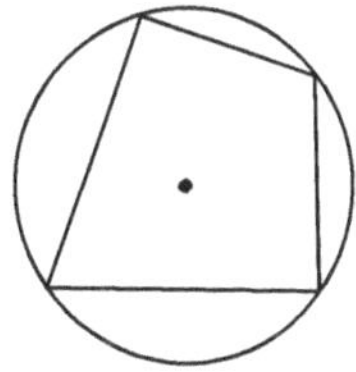

1.3 Inscribed circle: A circle, inside a polygon so that the circle touches all the sides of the polygon, is called **inscribed circle**. The centre of the circle is called **incentre** and the polygon is called **circumscribed polygon**. The following figures are examples of **inscribed circle**.

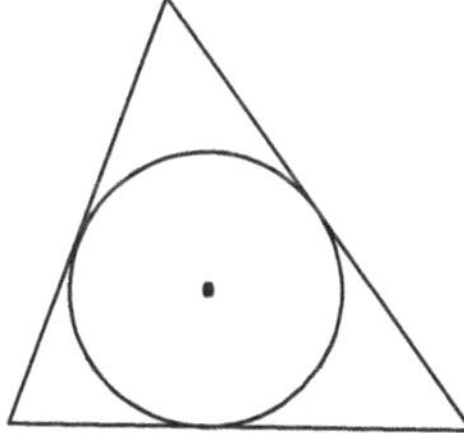 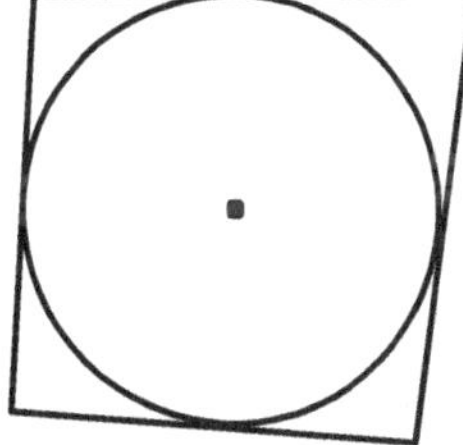

1.4 Tangent and secant: If a circle and a straight line lie in a plane, then with respect to each other one of the following three situations may exist:

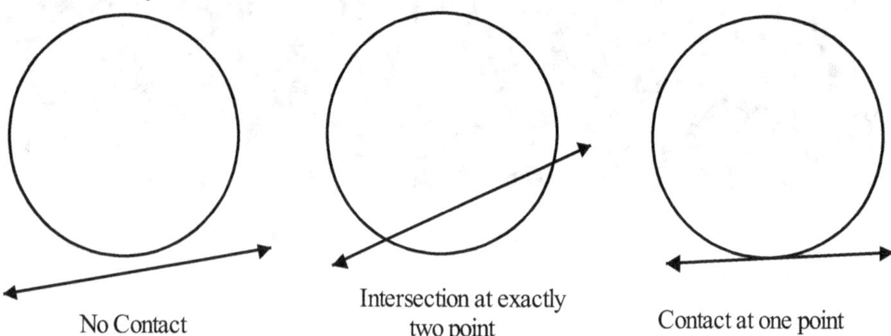

- The line is called **secant** if it intersects circle at two points
- The line which touches circle at one point is called the **tangent of the circle**.
- The point on the circumference, where the line touches is called the **point of contact**.

Remark:

(i) Through a point on the circle, there is one and only one tangent can pass.

(ii) Only two tangents can be drawn to a circle through a point outside the circle.

Theorem 1: The tangent at any point of a circle and the radius through the point are perpendicular to each other.

If we draw a number of line segment from the centre to the line, the perpendicular (OP here) is the shortest.

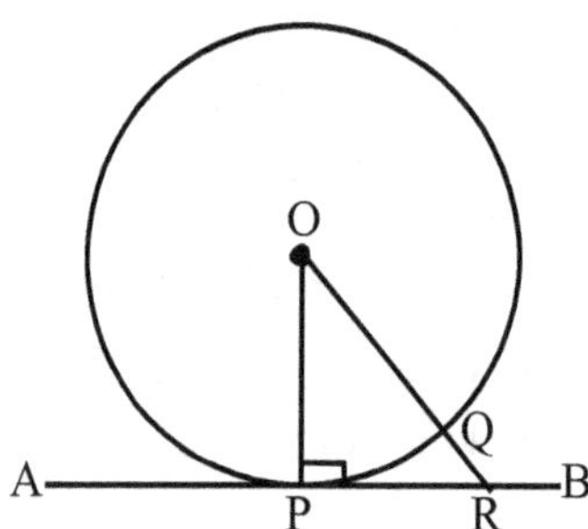

Solution:

Given: AB is a tangent at point P to a circle with centre O and radius OP.

To prove: OP $\perp$ AB

Construction: Take a point R other than P on AB, join OR which intersect the circle at Q.

Proof: OP $=$ OQ (radii)

$$OR = OQ + QR$$
$$OR > OQ$$
$$OR > OP (\because OP = OQ)$$

Thus, OP is shorter than any other line segment joining O to any point on AB.

$\therefore$ OP $\perp$ AB ($\because$ lines drawn from a point to line the perpendicular line segment is the shortest one).

Theorem 2: The length of tangents drawn from an external point to a circle are equal.

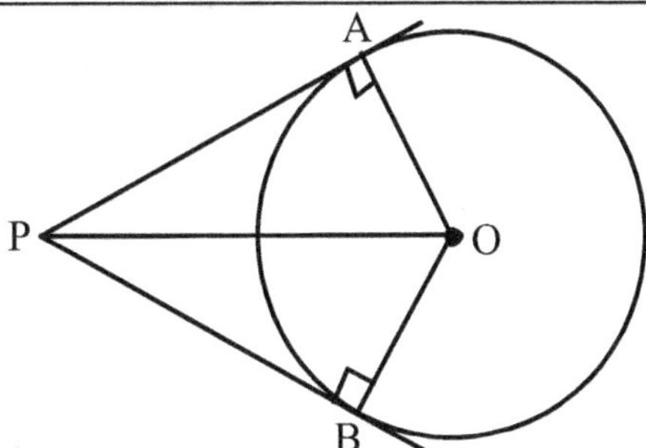

Solution:

Given: A circle with center O. PA and PB are tangents drawn from external point P to the circle.

To prove: $PA = PB$

Construction: Join OA, OB and OP.

Proof: We know that a tangent drawn from a point to a circle is perpendicular to the radius at the point of contact.

$\therefore$ OA $\perp$ AP and OB $\perp$ BP,

In $\triangle$OAP and $\triangle$OBP

$\angle A = \angle B$	(Each 90°)
OA = OB	(Radius)
OP = OP	(Common)
$\therefore \triangle$OAP $\cong \triangle$OBP	(By RHS)
So, PA = PB	(By CPCT)

Remark: Also proved that:

(i) The tangents subtend equal angles at the centre of the circle. $\angle$AOP = $\angle$BOP

(ii) The tangents are equally inclined to the line joining the point and the centre of the circle.

$\angle$APO = $\angle$BPO.

Practice Sheet - 1

Short questions (for one or two marks):

1. A line which is perpendicular to the radius of the circle through the point of contact is called a;

    (a) tangent   (b) chord   (c) normal   (d) segment

2. Number of tangents to a circle which are parallel to a secant is:

    (a) 1   (b) 2   (c) 3   (d) infinite

3. A line which intersects a circle at two distinct points is called:

    (a) tangent   (b) secant   (c) chord   (d) radius

4. The distance between two parallel tangents of a circle of radius 3 cm is:

    (a) 6 cm   (b) 3 cm   (c) 4.5 cm   (d) 12 cm

5. If the tangents from an external point are inclined at an angle of 70°, then the angle between the radii drawn through their points of contact is:

    (a) 35°   (b) 120°   (c) 110°   (d) 20°

6. In the figure, DE and DF are tangents from an external point D to a circle with centre A. If DE = 5 cm and DE ⊥ DF, then the radius of the circle is:

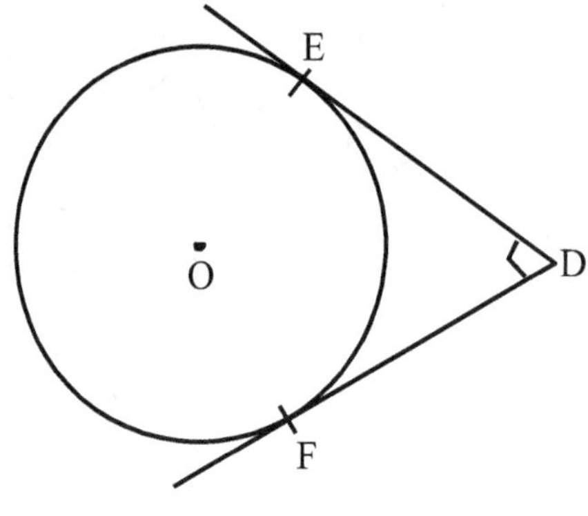

    (a) 3 cm   (b) 5 cm   (c) 4 cm   (d) 6 cm

7. ΔABC is isosceles with $AB = AC$. A circle touches all sides of the triangle, then which of the following is true?

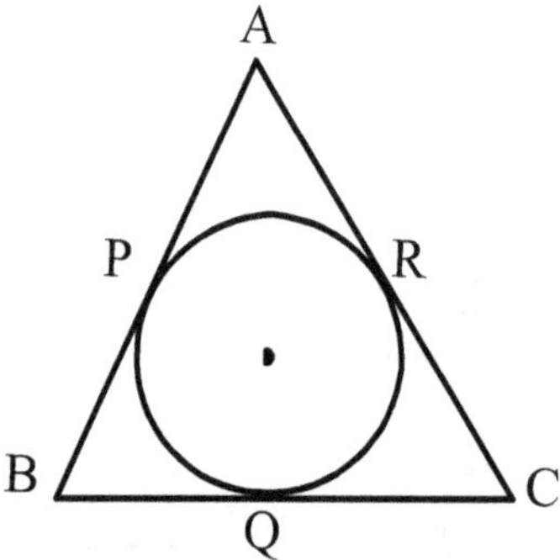

    (a) AB = BC   (b) BQ = QC   (c) BP = AP   (d) AR = RC

8. In the given figure, AQ, AR and BC are tangents to a circle with centre O. If AB = 7 cm, BC = 5 cm and AC = 5 cm, then length of the tangent AQ is:

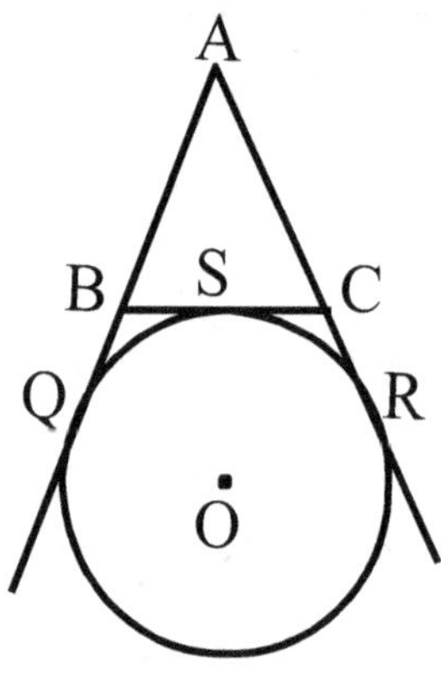

    (a) 5 cm   (b) 7 cm   (c) 8.5 cm   (d) 17 cm

9. PC is a tangent to the circle at C. AOB is the diameter which when extended meets the tangent at P. Find ∠CBA, ∠AOC, ∠BCO, if ∠PCA=110°.

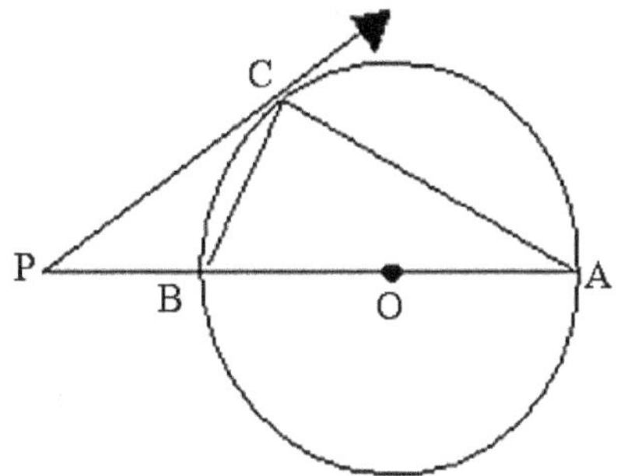

10. In the given figure, AD = 8 cm, AC = 6 cm and TB is the tangent at B to the circle with center O. Find OT, if BT is 4 cm.

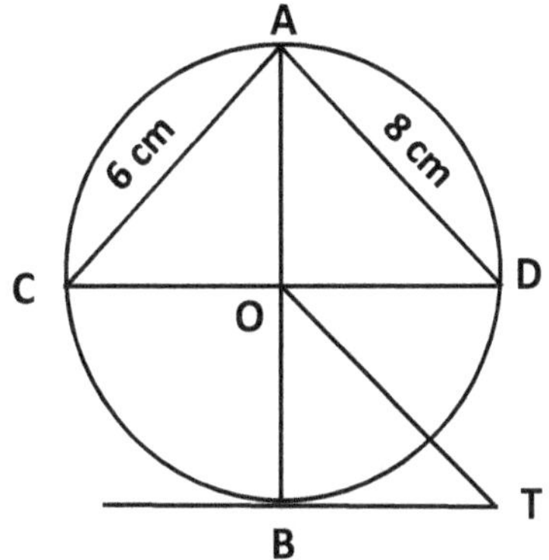

11. In the given figure, if angle OBC = 30°, then value of angle CAB.

    (a) 100°   (b) 110°   (c) 30°   (d) 15°

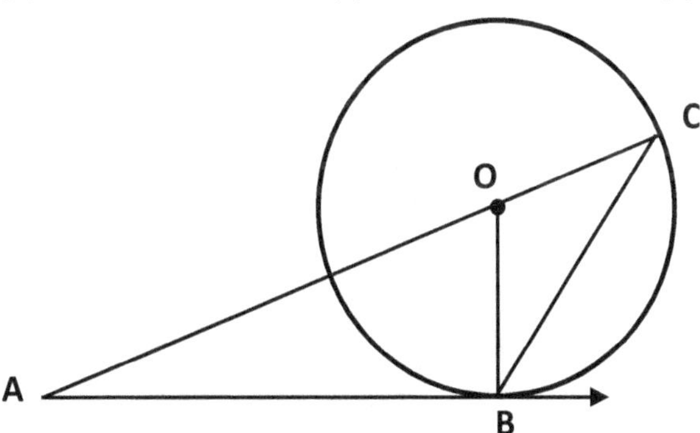

12. In the given figure, PQ is a chord of length 8 cm of a circle of radius 5 cm. The tangents at point P and Q intersect at point T. Find the length of tangent TP.

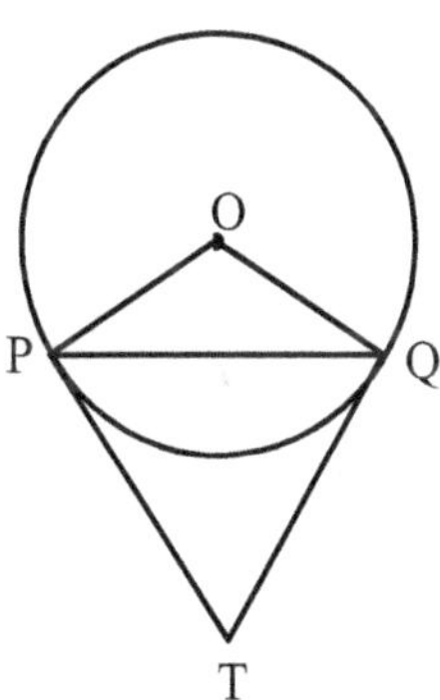

13. To circles with centers X and Y touch externally at P. If tangents AT and BT meet the common tangent at T, then prove that AT = BT.

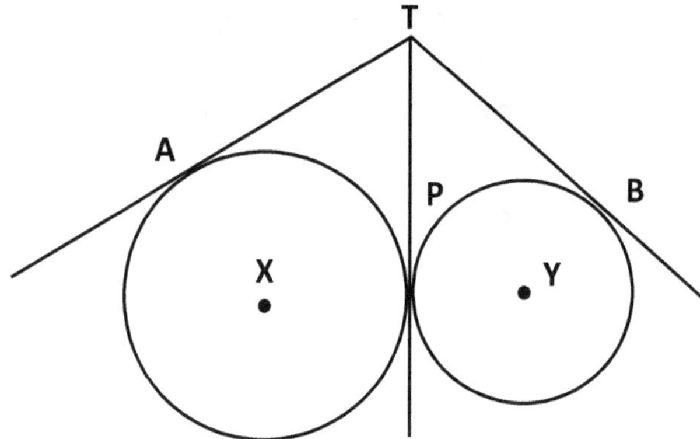

14. A tangent PA is drawn from an external point P to a circle of radius $3\sqrt{2}$ cm such that the distance of the point P from O is 6 cm as shown in the figure. The value of $\angle APO$.

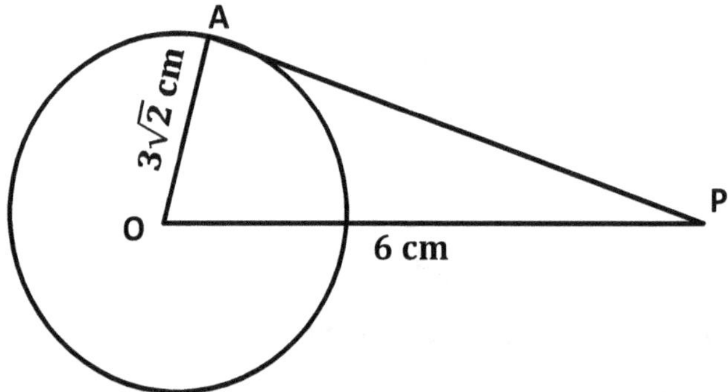

15. If in the isosceles triangle ABC of figure given below, AB = AC, show that BF = FC.

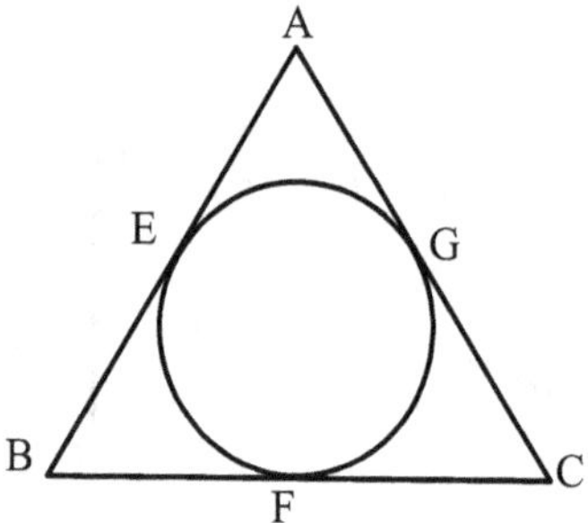

16. PA and PB are tangents from point P to the circle with centre O as shown in figure. At point M, a tangent is drawn cutting PA at K and PB at N. Prove that KN = AK + BN.

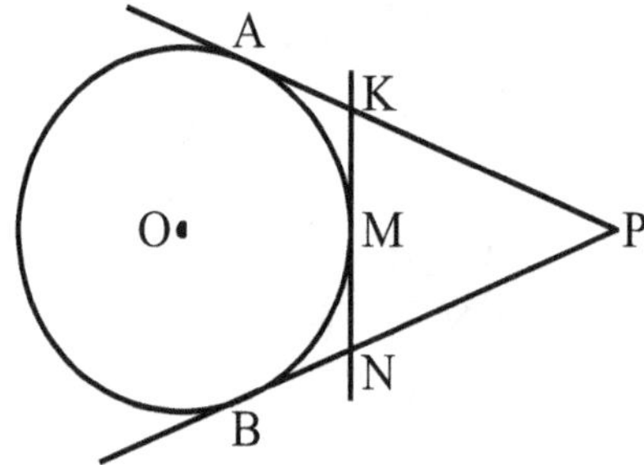

17. In the given figure, $\angle ADC = 90^o$, BC = 38 cm, CD = 28 cm and BP = 25 cm. Find the radius of the circle.

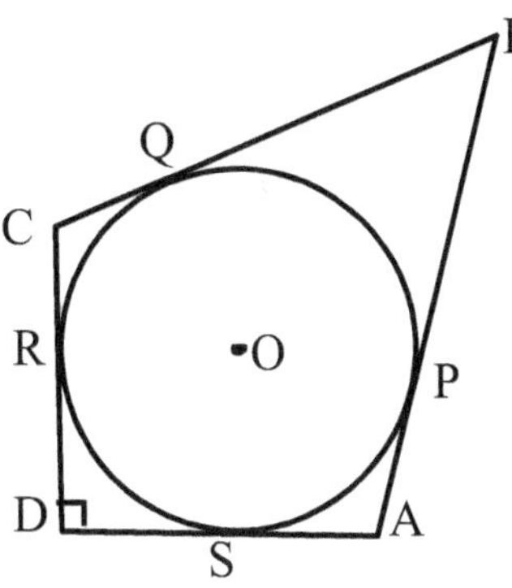

Three and four marks questions:

1. Find the length of tangent drawn to a circle with radius 5 cm from a point 13 cm away from the centre of the circle.

2. Prove that the angle between the two tangents to a circle drawn from an external point is supplementary to the angle subtended by the line segment joining the points of contact at the centre.

3. A circle is touching the side BC of triangle ABC at P and touching AB and AC produced at Q and R respectively. Prove that $AQ = \frac{1}{2} \times$ perimeter of triangle ABC.

4. From an external point P, two tangents PA and PB are drawn to a circle with centre O. If OP = 2OA, then show that triangle APB is equilateral.

5. In the given figure, two circles with centre A and B touch each other externally. PM = 15 cm is tangent to circle with centre A and QN = 13 cm is tangent to circle with centre B from external points P and Q. If PA = 17 cm and BQ = 12 cm, find the distance between the centers A and B of circles.

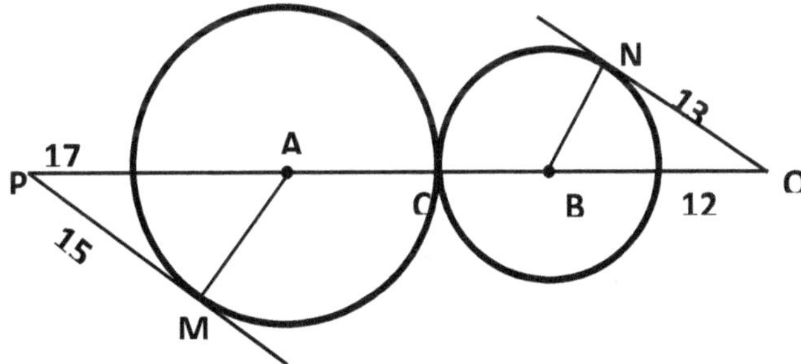

6. In the figure, the sides AB, BC and CA of triangle ABC touch a circle with centre O and radius r at P, Q and R respectively. Prove that:

(i) $AB + CQ = AC + BQ$ (ii) Area $(\triangle ABC) = \frac{1}{2}$ (perimeter of $\triangle ABC) \times r$

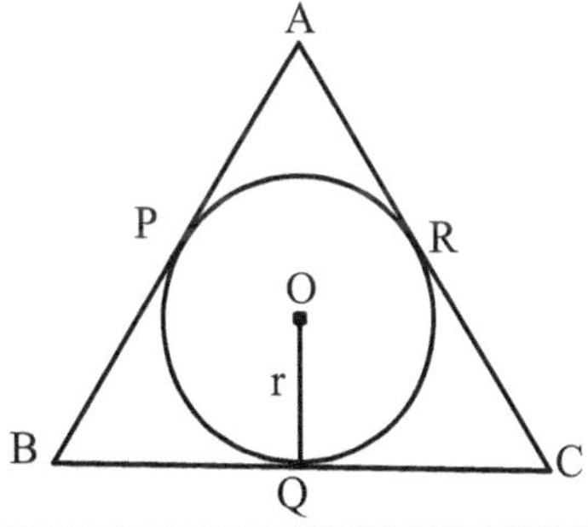

7. Prove that tangents to a circle from an external point are equal.

8. In the given figure, ΔABC is drawn to circumscribe a circle of radius 10 cm. Such that the segment BP and CP into which BC is divided by the point of contact P, are of lengths 15 cm and 20 cm respectively. If the area of $\Delta ABC = 525$ cm^2, then find the lengths of sides AB and AC.

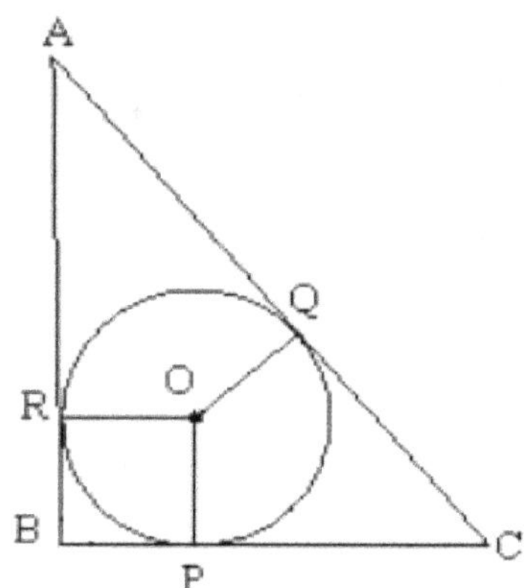

9. In figure given below, AB and CD are two common tangents of two circles with centers P and Q. These circles touch each other at M. If the common tangent at M meets AB and CD at X and Y respectively, prove that $XY = \frac{1}{2}(AB + CD)$.

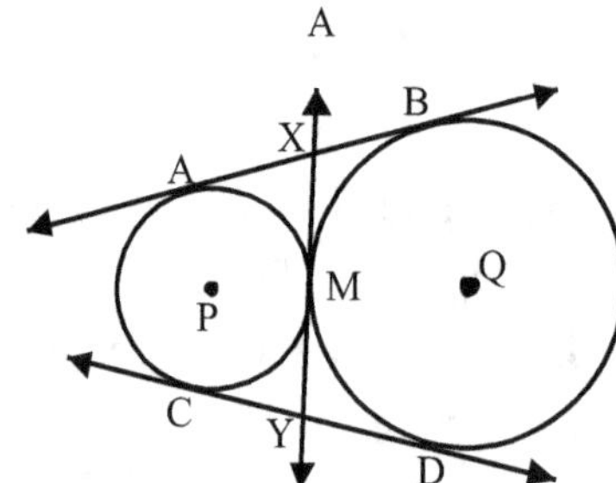

10. In the given figure, PQ is tangent at a point R of the circle with centre O. If $\angle TRQ = 30^{\circ}$ find $\angle PRS$.

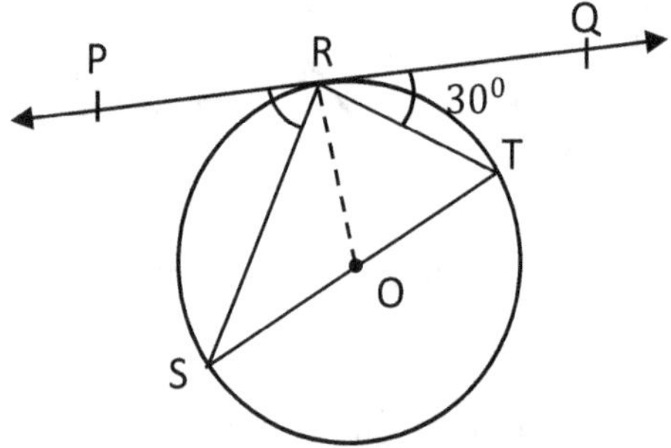

11. Prove that the parallelogram circumscribing a circle is a rhombus.

$$\boxed{\textbf{ANSWERS}}$$

Short questions (for one or two marks)	
Answer 1.	a
Answer 2.	b
Answer 3.	b
Answer 4.	a
Answer 5.	c
Answer 6.	b
Answer 7.	b
Answer 8.	c
Answer 9.	$70^\circ, 140^\circ, 70^\circ$
Answer 10.	$\sqrt{41}$ cm
Answer 11.	c
Answer 12.	$\dfrac{20}{3}$ cm
Answer 14.	45°
Answer 17.	15 cm
Three and four marks questions	
Answer 1.	12 cm
Answer 5.	13 cm
Answer 8.	AB = 32.5 cm, AC = 37.5 cm
Answer 10.	60°

Constructions

1.1 Introduction: In Construction we have already learned to construct angles (30°, 45°, 60°, 75°, 90°, 105°, 120°, 135° etc). We have learned how to bisect an angle, drawing the perpendicular bisector of a line segment etc. Here we will learn how to **divide a line segment in a given ratio** (internally) and **tangent to a given circle** from a point outside it. Lets' recall some basic constructions first:

1.2 Construction of bisector of a given angle:

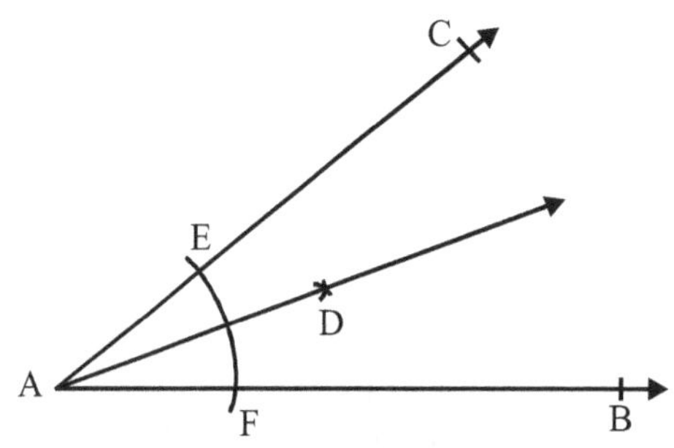

Steps:

1. Draw an angle∠BAC (any measurement).
2. With A as centre draw an arc (any radius) which intersect AC at E and AB at F.
3. With E as centre, draw an arc (More than half of EF).
4. With F as centre and same radius as in step 3, draw another arc which intersect the arc in step 3 at a point named D.
5. Join AD and produce it. This ray AD is the required bisector of ∠BAC.

1.3 Construction of perpendicular bisector or a given line segment

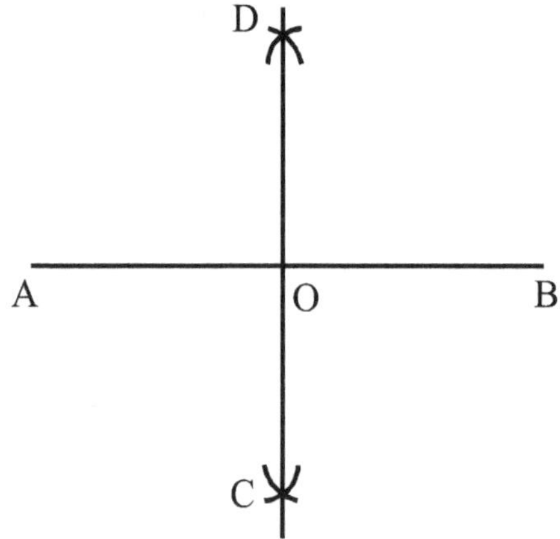

Steps:

1. Draw a line segment AB.
2. With A and B as centre and radius equal to more than half of AB, draw arcs on both sides of line segment AB.
3. These arcs intersect at point C and D as shown in figure.

4. Join CD. CD intersects AB at point O. Then line CD is the required perpendicular
   bisector of line segment AB.

1.4 Draw a line parallel to a given line:

In the following figure l is a given line segment. We have to draw a line parallel to it.

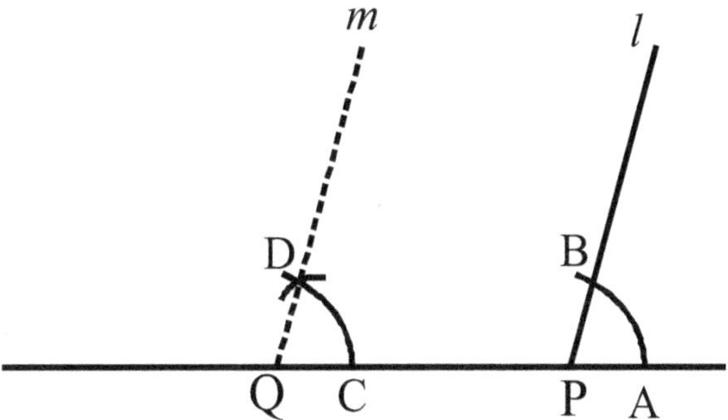

Steps:

1. With P as centre mark an arc AB (any radius).
2. With Q as centre mark an equal arc.
3. Measure arc AB and through C mark an arc (equal to AB), which intersect the previous arc at D. Join QD
   and produce it.
4. Then $l \parallel m$ (as corresponding angles are equal).

1.5 To divide a line segment in a given ratio:

Given a line segment AB. Divide it in the ratio m: n, where both m and n are positive integers. To understand
this construction, take m = 3 and n = 4.

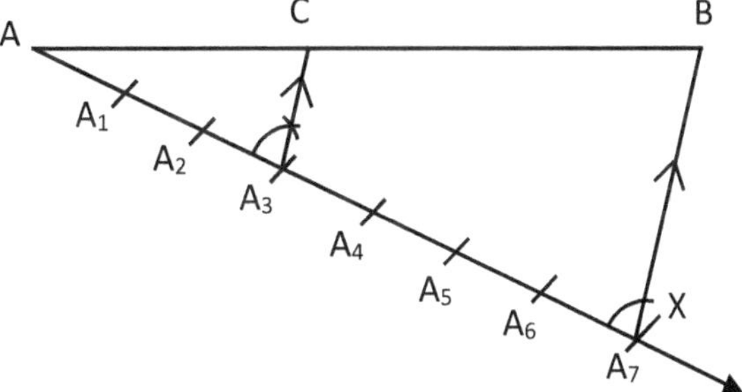

Steps:

1. Draw a line segment AB = 10 cm.
2. Draw a ray AX making an acute angle with AB.
3. Locate 7 points A_1, A_2, A_3, A_4, A_5, A_6 and A_7 on AX , so that $AA_1 = A_1A_2 = A_2A_3 = A_3A_4 = A_4A_5 = A_5A_6$
   $= A_6A_7$.
4. Join BA_7.
5. Through the point A_3 draw $A_3C \parallel BA_7$ meet AB at C.
6. Now AC: CB = 3: 4.

1.6 Tangents to a circle from a point outside it:

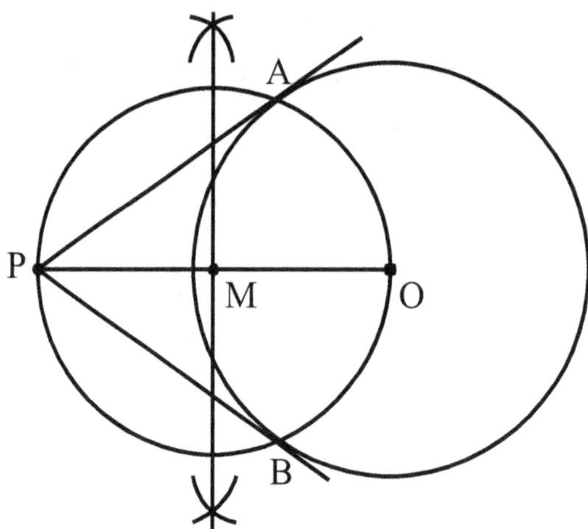

Steps:

1. Draw a given circle with centre O and mark a point P outside it at a given distance.
2. Join OP and bisect it (draw perpendicular bisector of OP).Let M is the midpoint of OP.
3. With M as centre and MP as radius draw a circle, which intersect the given circle at A and B.
4. Join PA and PB.
5. Then PA and PB are the required tangents.

Practice Sheet

Multiple choice questions:

1. In the given figure P divides AB internally in the ratio:

   (a)3: 4   (b) 4: 3   (c) 3: 7   (d) 4: 7

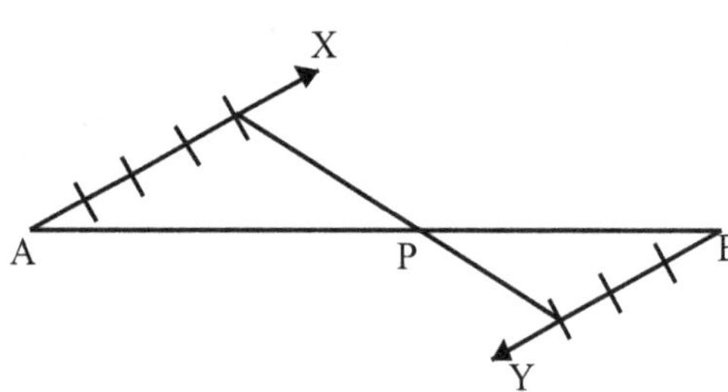

2. To divide a line segment AB in the ratio 4 : 5, a ray AX is drawn first such that $\angle$BAX is an acute angle and then points A_1, A_2, A_3, . . . are located at equal distances on the ray AX and the point B is joined to:

   (a) A_{10} (b) A_{12} (c) A_9 (d) A_7

3. To draw a pair of tangents to a circle which are inclined to each other at an angle of 60°, it is required to draw tangents at end points of those two radii of the circle, the angle between them should be:

   (a) 60°   (b) 90°   (c) 120°   (d) 135°

4. By geometrical constructions, it is not possible to divide a line segment in the ratio:

   (a) 1: 3   (b) 2: 3   (c) $2 - \sqrt{5} : 2 + \sqrt{5}$ (d) 5: 7

5. To locate a point Q on PR such that QR = $\dfrac{2}{3}$ PQ, line segment PR should be divided in the ratio:

(a) 2: 3   (b) 2: 5   (c) 3: 2   (d) 5: 2

6. To draw two tangents to a circle of radius 3 cm and centre O from a point P, 8 cm away from O, we draw a circle with centre at the mid – point of OP and radius equal to:

(a) 8 cm   (b) 3 cm   (c) 5 cm   (d) 4 cm

Three and four marks questions:

1. Draw a line segment of length 7.6 cm and divide it in the ratio 5: 8. Measure the two parts.

2. Draw a circle of radius 6 cm. From a point 10 cm away from its centre, construct the pair of tangents to the circle and measure their lengths.

3. Draw a line segment AB = 7 cm. Taking A as center, draw a circle of radius 3 cm. From point B, construct a pair of tangents to the circle with centre A.

4. Construct two tangents PT and PQ to a circle of radius 4 cm and centre O such that $\angle TOQ = 120^o$.

5. Draw two circles of radius 3.5 cm and 5.5 cm which are 8 cm apart from their center. Now from the center of the bigger circle, construct a pair of tangents to the smaller circle.

6. Construct a tangent to a circle of radius 4 cm from a point on the concentric circle of radius 6 cm and measure its length.

$$\boxed{\textbf{ANSWERS}}$$

Multiple choice questions	
Answer 1.	b
Answer 2.	c
Answer 3.	c
Answer 4.	c
Answer 5.	c
Answer 6.	d
Three and four marks questions	
Answer 1.	2.9 cm and 4.7 cm
Answer 2.	8 cm each
Answer 6.	4.4 cm (approx)

Heights and Distances

1.1 Introduction: Using Trigonometrical ratios we can find the missing sides of a triangle. Using the same concept, we can find the heights or distances of some real-life objects, like height of a building, a hill etc. **Heights and Distances** is one of the most important applications of Trigonometry.

Line of sight: To understand the line of sight consider two situations given below:

(i) A person standing at A (at some distance from the foot of a tower) and is looking at the top of the tower (Figure – 1)

(ii) A Person standing at the top of the tower and looking at an object at point A (Figure – 2).

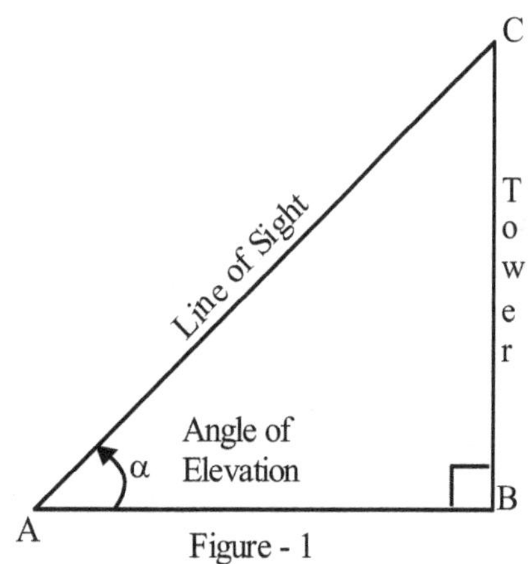

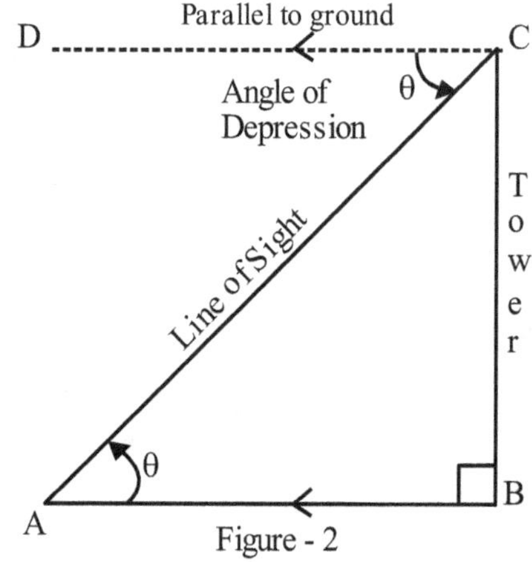

1.2 Angle of Elevation: The angle made by the line of sight with the horizontal when a person raise his head to see the top of a tower **C** is called **angle of elevation**. In the figure – 1 given above $\angle BAC$ is the angle of elevation.

1.3 Angle of Depression: The angle made by the line of sight with the horizontal when a person down his head to see the point at A (at some distance from the foot of the tower) is called **angle of depression**. In the figure – 2 given above $\angle DCA$ is the angle of depression, which in turn equals to the angle of elevation. So $\angle DCA = \angle BAC$ (alternate).

Angle of elevation = Angle of depression

Remark:

1. Use required trigonometrical ratio with angle of elevation or depression to find the unknown quantity.

2. Heights and distances is completely based on **diagram**. Focus on making diagram according to question. Calculation is secondary.

Multiple choice questions:

1. A ladder 15 m long just reaches the top of a vertical wall. If the ladder makes an angle of 60° with the wall, then the height of the wall is:

   (a) $15\sqrt{3}$ m   (b) $\dfrac{15\sqrt{3}}{2}$ m   (c) $\dfrac{15}{2}$ m   (d) 15 m

2. If the altitude of the sun is at 30°, then the height of the vertical tower that will cast a shadow of length 30 m on the ground is:

   (a) $10\sqrt{3}$m   (b) 10 m   (c) $30\sqrt{3}$ m   (d) 30 m

3. A kite is flying at a height of 30 m above the ground. The string attached to the kite is temporarily tied to the ground. If the inclination of the string with the ground is 60°, then the length of the string assuming that there is no slack in the string is:

   (a) $20\sqrt{3}$ m   (b) 20 m   (c) 60 m   (d) $30\sqrt{2}$ m

4. If the height and length of the shadow of a man are the same, then the angle of elevation of the sun is:

   (a) 30°   (b) 60°   (c) 45°   (d) 15°

5. If two towers of height h_1 and h_2 subtend angles of 60° and 30° respectively at the midpoint of the line segment joining their feet, then $h_1 : h_2$ is:

   (a) 3 : 1   (b) $\sqrt{3} : 1$ (c) $1 : \sqrt{3}$ (d) 1 : 3

6. An observer 1.5 m tall is 28.5 m away from a tower 30 m high. The angle of elevation of the top of the tower from his eye is:

   (a) 30°   (b) 45°   (c) 60°   (d) 90°

7. In the given figure, ABCD is a rectangle with AD = 12 cm and DC = 20 cm, line segment DE is drawn making an angle of 30° with AD, intersecting AB in E. The length of DE is:

   (a) $4\sqrt{3}$ cm   (b) $8\sqrt{3}$ cm   (c) 12 cm   (d) 24 cm

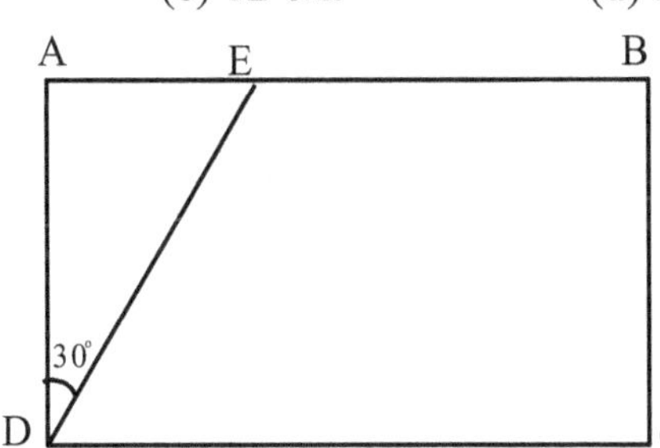

Short and Long answer type questions:

1. A tower is 100 m high. Find the angle of elevation of its top from a point 100 m away from its foot.

2. A kite flying at a height of 75 m from the level ground is attached to a straight string inclined at 60° to the horizontal ground. Find the length of the string to the nearest meter.

3. From the top of a tower, a man finds that the angle of depression of a car on the ground is 30°. If the car is at a distance 40 m away from the tower, find the height of the tower in nearest meter.

4. From a point P on level ground, the angle of elevation of the top of a tower is 30°. If the tower is 100 m high, how far is P from the foot of the tower?

5. A pole being broken by the wind, the top struck the ground at an angle of 30° and at a distance of 8 m from the foot of the pole. Find the whole height of the pole?

6. A ladder rests against a vertical wall such that the top of the ladder reahes the top of the wall. The ladder is inclined at 60° with the ground, and the bottom of the ladder is 1.5 m away from the foot of the wall. Find:
(i) The length of the ladder
(ii) The height of the wall

7. A tower is 64 m tall. A man standing erect at a distance of 36 m from the tower observes the angle of elevation of the top of the tower to be 60°. Find the height of the man.

8. From the top of a cliff 150 m high, the angles of depression of two boats are 60° and 30°. Find the distance between the boats, if the boats are:
(i) On the same sides of the cliff.
(ii) On the opposite sides of the cliff.

9. From a point on the ground 40 m away from the foot of a tower, the angle of elevation of the top of the tower is 30°. The angle of elevation to the top of a water tank (on the top of the tower) is 45°. Find the:
(i)   Height of the tower
(ii) The depth of the tank

10. A person standing on the bank of a river observes that the angle of elevation of the top of a tree standing on the opposite bank is 60°. When he retreats 40 m away from the bank, he finds that the angle of elevation to be 30°. Find:
(i) The height of the tree
(ii) The width of the river, correct to two decimal places

11. From the top of a cliff 90 m high, the angles of depression of the top and bottom of a tower are observed to be 30° and 60° respectively. Find the height of tower.

12. The angle of elevation of a jet plane from a point A on the ground is 60°. After flight of 15 seconds, the angle of elevation changes to 30°. If the jet plane is flying at a constant height of $1500\sqrt{3}$ m, find the speed of the jet plane.

13. The angle of elevation of the top Q of a vertical tower PQ from a point X on the ground is 60°. At a point Y, 40 m vertically above X, the angle of elevation is 45°. Find the height of the tower PQ and the distance XQ.

14. The angle of elevation of a cloud from a point h meter above a lake is 30° and the angle of depression of the reflection of cloud in the lake is 45°. If the height of the cloud be 200 m. Find h.

15. The angle of elevation from a point P of the top of a tower QR, 50m high is 60° and that of the tower PT from a point Q is 30°. Find the height of the towcr PT, correct to the nearest meter.

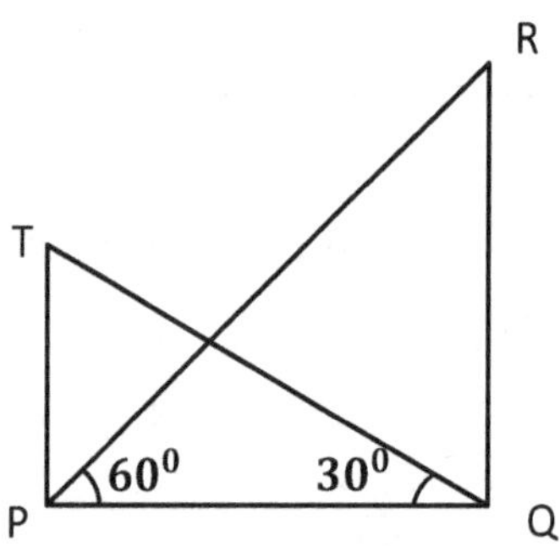

16. A man observes the angle of elevation of the top of the tower to be 45°. He walks towards it in a horizontal line through its base. On covering 20 m the angle of elevation changes to 60°. Find the height of the tower correct to two significant figures.

17. From the top of a cliff, the angle of depression of the top and bottom of a tower are observed to be 45° and 60° respectively. If the height of the tower is 20 m. Find:
(i) The height of the cliff.
(ii) The distance between the cliff and the tower.

18. The angle of elevation of the top of a tower from two points P and Q at distances a and b respectively, from the base and in the same straight line with it, are complementary. Prove that the height of the tower is $\sqrt{ab}$.

19. From the top of the tower the angle of depression of an object on the horizontal ground is found to be 60°. On descending 20 m vertically downwards from the top of the tower, the angle of depression of the object is found to be 30°. Find the height of the tower.

20. A vertical tower stands on a horizontal plane and is surmounted by a vertical flagstaff of height h meter. At a point on the plane, the angle of elevation of the bottom of the flagstaff is α and that of the top of flagstaff is β. Prove that the height of the tower is: $\dfrac{h \tan \alpha}{\tan \beta - \tan \alpha}$.

21. The angle of elevation of the top of a building from the foot of the tower is 30° and the angle of elevation of the top of the tower from the foot of the building is 60°. If the tower is 60 m high, find the height of the building.

ANSWERS

Multiple choice questions	
Answer 1.	c
Answer 2.	a
Answer 3.	a
Answer 4.	c
Answer 5.	a
Answer 6.	b
Answer 7.	b
Short and long answer type questions	
Answer 1.	60°
Answer 2.	87 m
Answer 3.	23 m
Answer 4.	173.2 m
Answer 5.	13.86 m
Answer 6.	(i) 3m (ii) 2.6 m
Answer 7.	1.65 m
Answer 8.	(i) 173.2 m (ii) 346.4 m
Answer 9.	(i) 23.1 m (approx.) (ii) 16.9 m (approx.)
Answer 10.	(i) 34.64 m (ii) 20 m
Answer 11.	60 m
Answer 12.	720 km/hr
Answer 13.	94.64 m, 109.3 m
Answer 14.	53.6 m
Answer 15.	16.67m
Answer 16.	47 m
Answer 17.	27.32 m
Answer 19.	30 m
Answer 21.	20 m

Surface Area and Volume

1.1 Introduction: We see many objects/articles around us. These objects can be categorized into two categories:

(i) Two dimensional or 2D: These are also called **plane figure** that has no thickness. They lie entirely in **one plane**. These objects can be composed of line segments, curves or a combination of the two. They occupy space in one plane only, so we can calculate their **area** and **perimeter**. **For example:** circle triangle, quadrilateral etc.

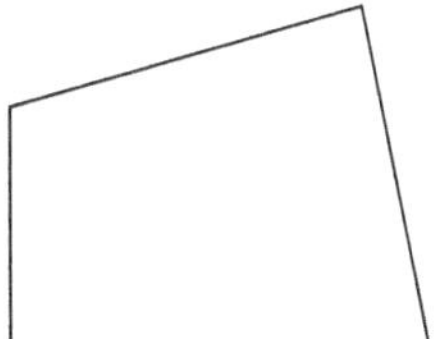 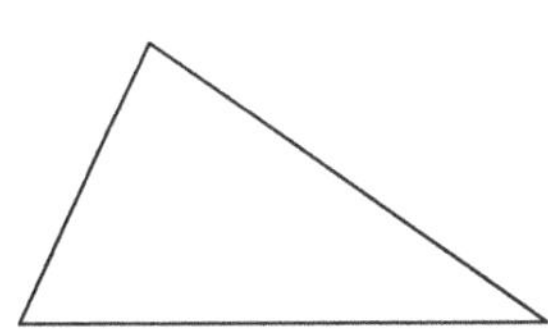 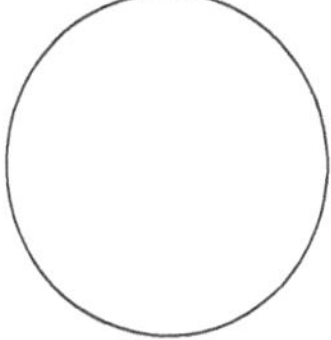

(ii) Three dimensional or 3D: These are also called **solids**, or we can say **2D figure with thickness/height**. They occupy space in two planes so we can determine their **surface area** and **volume**. **For example:** cylinder, cone, sphere, cuboids, cube and hemisphere etc. You have learnt how to calculate surface area and volumes of these solids. Let's recall formulae for each solids:

 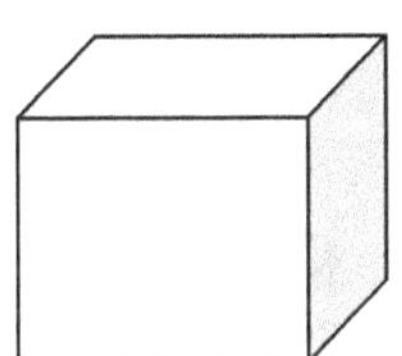

Formulae:

1.2 Cube and Cuboids: Let dimension of the cuboids are length (**l**), breadth (**b**) and height (**h**) and sides of cube are **a** unit.

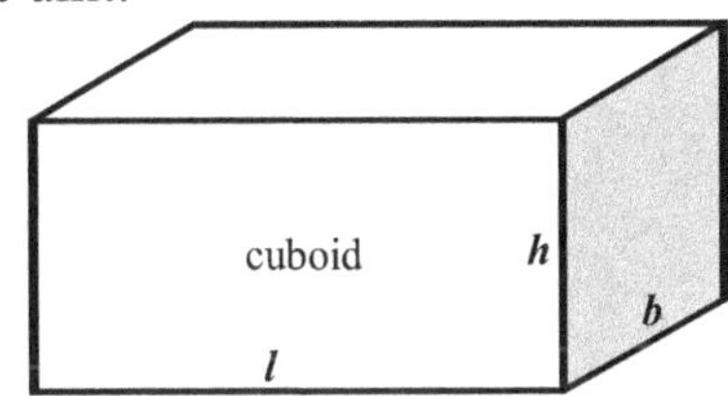

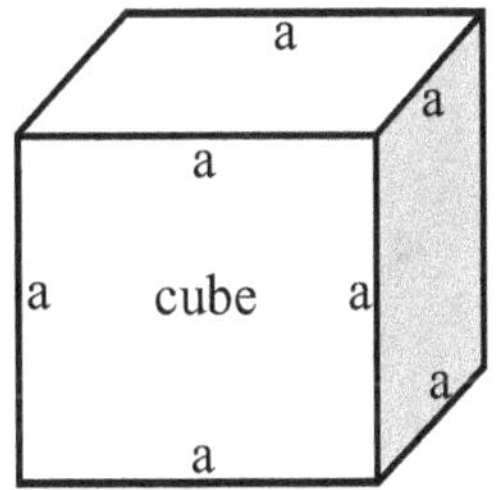

	Cuboid	**Cube**
Volume	$l \times b \times h$	a^3
Lateral surface area (area of 4 walls)	$2h(l + b)$	$4a^2$
Total surface area (area of six surfaces)	$2(lb + bh + hl)$	$6a^2$
Diagonal	$\sqrt{l^2 + b^2 + h^2}$	$a\sqrt{3}$

1.3 Solid cylinder: Let r be the radius and **h** be the height of a solid right circular cylinder, then:

(i) Curved (lateral) surface area or area of walls = perimeter of cross section $\times$ height = $2\pi rh$ (unit^2)

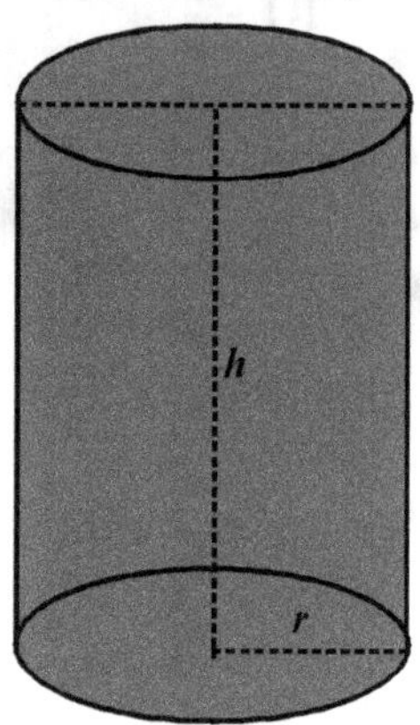

(ii) Total surface area = curved surface area + area of both circular ends

$$= 2\pi rh + 2\pi r^2$$
$$= 2\pi r(h + r) \text{ (unit}^2)$$

(iii) Volume = area of cross section $\times$ height

$$= \pi r^2 h \text{ (unit}^3)$$

1.4 Hollow Cylinder (Pipe): There are two cylinders whose height is same and radius of outer (R) > radius of inner (r). There are total 4 surfaces. 1 inner curved surface, 1 outer curved surface, two rings.

(i) Thickness of cylinder = R − r

(ii) Area of cross section (Ring) = $\pi(R^2 - r^2)$

(iii) External curved surface area = $2\pi Rh$

(iv) Internal curved surface area = $2\pi rh$

(v) Total surface area = External CSA + Internal CSA + area of both rings.

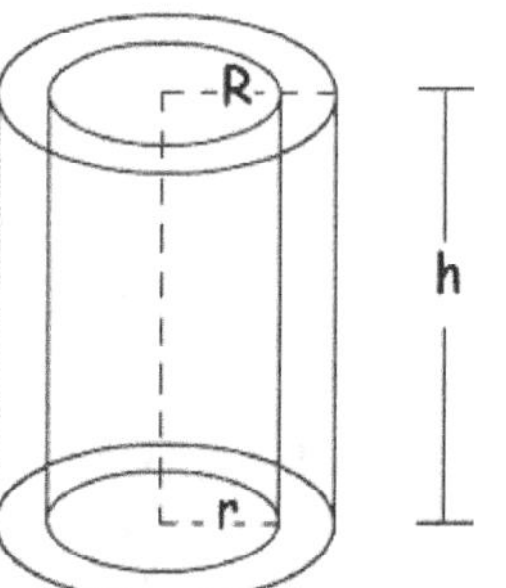

$$= 2\pi Rh + 2\pi rh + 2\pi(R^2 - r^2)$$

(vi) Volume of material = Volume of external cylinder (material + air) − volume of internal cylinder (air)

$$= \pi R^2 h - \pi^2 h$$
$$= \pi(R^2 - r^2)h$$

1.5 Cone: Let r be the radius of circular base, **h** be the vertical height and **l** being the slant height:

(i) Slant height $l = \sqrt{h^2 + r^2}$

(ii) Curved surface area (CSA) = πrl

(iii) Total surface area (TSA) = CSA + area of base

$$= \pi rl + \pi r^2$$
$$= \pi r(l + r)$$

(iv) Volume $= \dfrac{1}{3}\pi r^2 h$

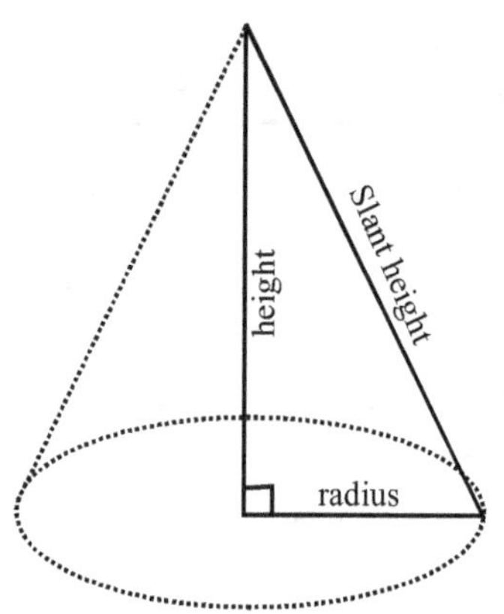

1.6 Sphere: Let r be the radius of spherical ball. Sphere has only one surface.

(i) Volume of sphere $= \dfrac{4}{3}\pi r^3$

(ii) Curved surface area = Total surface area = $4\pi r^2$

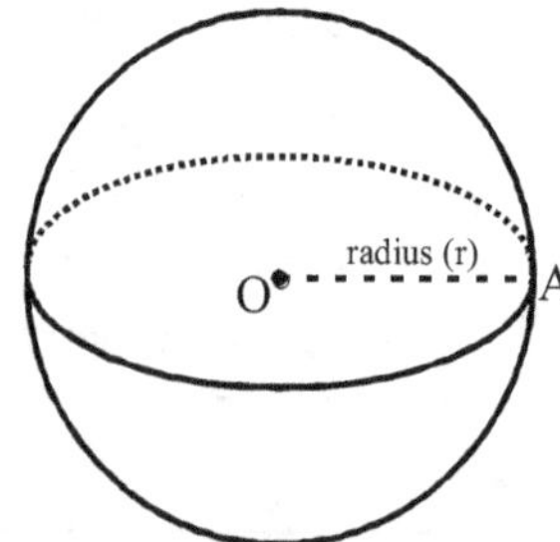

1.7 Hemisphere: Half sphere is hemisphere. Its base could be solid (like half lemon) or hollow (like half coconut)

(i) Volume $= \frac{2}{3}\pi r^3$ (ii) Curved surface area $= 2\pi r^2$ (iii) Total surface area $= 3\pi r^2$	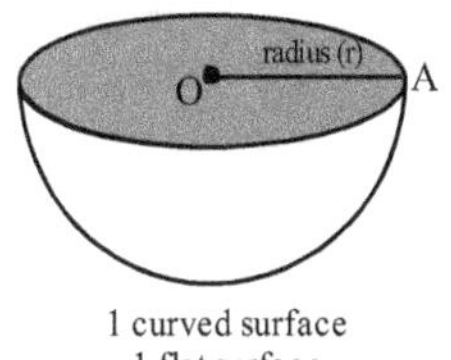 1 curved surface 1 flat surface
(i) Volume of material $= \frac{2}{3}\pi R^3 - \frac{2}{3}\pi r^3$ (ii) Width of ring $= R - r$ (iii) Inner CSA $= 2\pi r^2$ (iv) Outer CSA $= 2\pi R^2$ (v) Total surface area $=$ Outer CSA + Inner CSA + area of ring $= 2\pi R^2 + 2\pi r^2 + \pi(R^2 - r^2)$	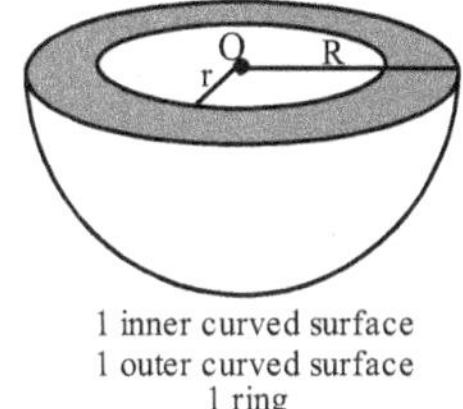 1 inner curved surface 1 outer curved surface 1 ring

1.8 Cross Section of a solid: Every solid has a plane figure in its base, which is called **cross section**. For example cylinders and cones have a circular cross section, cubes and cuboids have a quadrilateral (Rectangle or square) cross section etc.

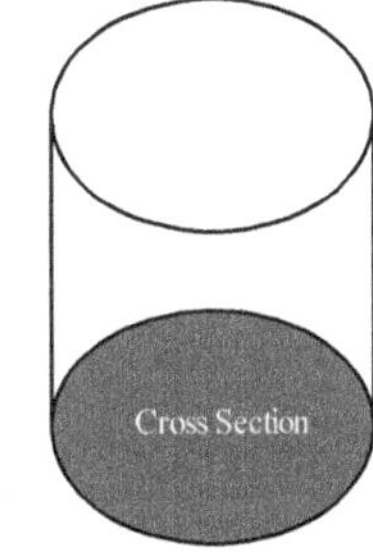

1.9 Surface area and volume of combination of solids: In our daily life we come across a number of solids made of combinations of two or more solids.

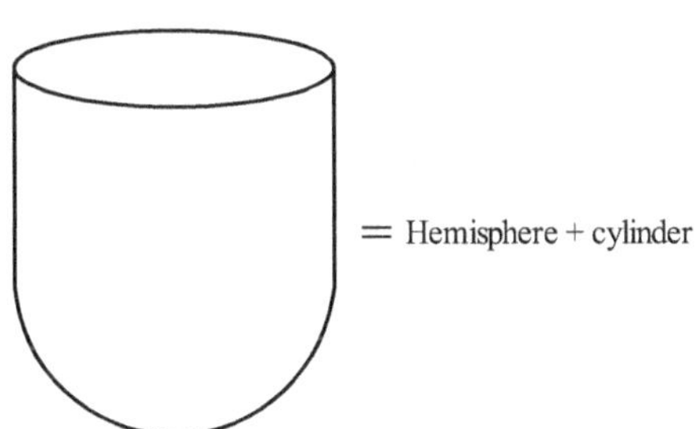

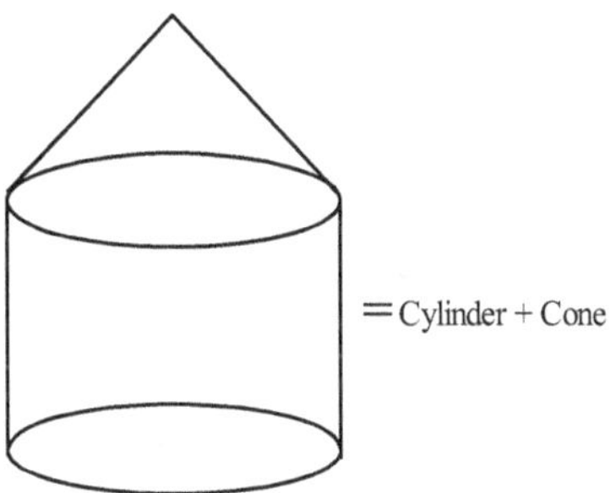

For Example: In the combinations given below a closed cone has 2 surfaces (1 flat and 1 curved) and a closed cylinder has 3 surfaces (2 flat and 1 curved) so there are total 5 surfaces. But when we combined them there are only 3 surfaces: 1 flat surface of cylinder,1 curved surface of cylinder and 1 curved surface of cone.

Volume of combined solid = Volume of cylinder + Volume of cone

$$= \pi r^2 h + \frac{1}{3}\pi r^2 h$$

Surface area of combined solid = Area of circular base of cylinder + CSA of cylinder + CSA of cone

$$= \pi r^2 + 2\pi rh + \pi rl$$

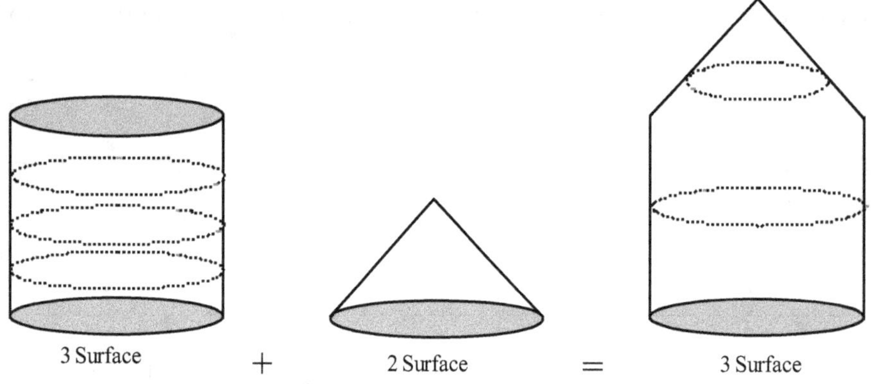

Remark: To find surface area and volume of such combinations we have formulas. But be careful while applying them. Because while calculating volume it is easy to say that **volume of whole solid = volume of solid 1 $\pm$ volume of solid 2**, but **while calculating surface area, it is not that straight**. Because when two or more solids combined, their surfaces overlap each other and may be **vanished**.

1.10 Conversion of solid from one shape to another:

(i) When a solid melts and recast into another solid, its volume remain same.

(ii) When a big solid melts and recast into number of small solids then:

$$\text{Number of small solids formed} = \frac{\text{Volume of big solid}}{\text{Volume of 1 small solid}}$$

Remark: Do not take $\pi = 3.14$ unless stated. Take it $\pi = \dfrac{22}{7}$.

Practice Sheet

Short Questions for one or two marks:

1. A test tube used in lab has the shape of the combination of:

    (a) A cone and a cylinder   (b) A cone and a hemisphere

    (c) A cylinder and a sphere   (d) A cylinder and hemisphere

2. The curved surface area of a right circular cone of height 15 cm and base diameter 16 cm is:

    (a) $60\pi\ \text{cm}^2$ (b) $68\pi\ \text{cm}^2$ (c) $120\pi\ \text{cm}^2$ (d) $136\pi\ \text{cm}^2$

3. The ratio of the total surface area of a solid hemisphere to the square of its radius:

    (a) $2\pi:1$ (b) $3\pi:1$ (c) $4\pi:1$ (d) $1:4\pi$

4. The radius of the largest right circular cone that can be cut out from a cube of edge 4.2 is:

    (a) 5.2 cm   (b) 8.4 cm   (c) 1.05 cm   (d) 2.1 cm

5. Three cubes each of volume 216 cm³ are joined end to end. The dimensions of the resulting solid are:

    (a) $6 \times 6 \times 6$ (b) $18 \times 18 \times 6$ (c) $18 \times 6 \times 6$ (d) $8 \times 6 \times 6$

6. If the surface area of two spheres is in the ratio 16: 9, then their volumes will be in the ratio:

    (a) 27: 64   (b) 64: 27   (c) 4: 3   (d) 3: 4

7. How many spherical bolls, each of radiuses 1 cm, can be made from a solid sphere of lead of radius 8 cm.

(a) 256   (b) 512   (c) 1024   (d) 576

8. A toy is in the form of a right circular cylinder surmounted by a right circular cone as shown in the figure. If AD = DE = DC = 1 cm, the volume of toy in cm^3 is:

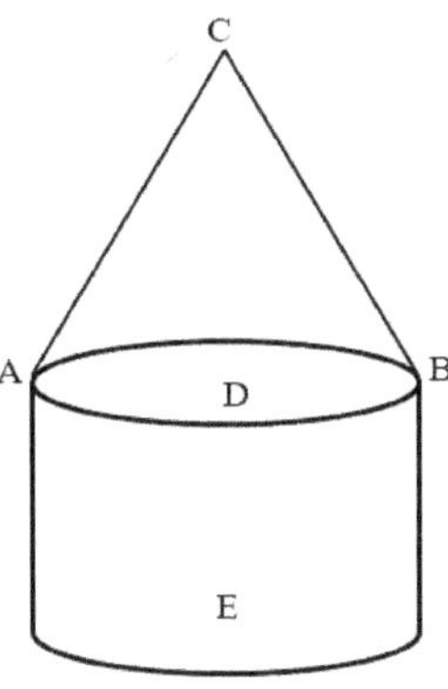

(a) $\dfrac{4}{3}\pi$ (b) $\dfrac{3}{4}\pi$ (c) 3π (d) 4π

9. Volume of two cubes is in the ratio of 8: 125. The ratio of their surface area is:

     (a) 2: 5   (b) 4: 25   (c) 16: 25   (d) 8: 125

10. Twelve solid sphere of same size are made by melting a solid metallic cylinder of base diameter 2 cm and height 16 cm. The diameter of each sphere is:

     (a) 2 cm   (b) 3 cm   (c) 4 cm   (d) 6 cm

11. The number of cubes of side 2 cm which can be cut from a cube of side 6 cm is:

     (a) 56   (b) 54   (c) 28   (d) 27

12. The total surface area of a right circular cone is $90\pi\,\text{cm}^2$. If the radius of the base of the cone is 5 cm, find the height of the cone.

13. Three cubes each of side 15 cm are joined end to end. Find the total surface area of the resulting cuboid.

14. A vessel is in the form of a hollow hemisphere mounted by a hollow cylinder. The diameter of the hemisphere is 14 cm and the total height of the vessel is 13 cm. Find the inner surface area of the vessel. (Take $\pi = \dfrac{22}{7}$)

15. The radius and slant height of a right circular cone are in the ratio of 7: 13 and its curved surface area is 286 cm^2. Find the radius of the cone. (Take $\pi = \dfrac{22}{7}$)

Three and four marks questions:

1. A solid right circular copper cone of height 15 cm and radius 6 cm is melted, and smaller copper cones of height 3 cm and radius 2 cm are made. How many smaller cones can be made?

2. A solid metallic right cone is melted and a number of solid right cylinders are made with the material. Find the number of cylinders if the radius of the base of each cylinder is half the radius of the cone and the height of each cylinder is one-third the height of the cone.

3. A conical hole in drilled in a circular cylinder of height 12 cm and base radius 5 cm. The height and base radius of the cone is also the same. Find the whole surface and volume of the remaining portion of cylinder.

4. If the diameter of the cross-section of a wire is decreased by 5%, how much percent will the length be increased so that the volume remains the same.

5. The volume of a conical tent is 1232 m^3 and the area of the bare floor is 154 m^2.

Calculate the:
(i) Radius of the floor.
(ii) Height of the tent.
(iii) Length of the canvas required to cover this conical tent if its width is 2 m.

6. A vessel in the form of an inverted cone is filled with water to the brim. Its height is 20 cm and diameter is 16.8 cm. Two equal solid cones are dropped in it so that they are fully submerged. As a result, one third of the water in the original cone overflows. What is the volume of each of the solid cones submerged?

7. A circus tent is in the shape of a cylinder surmounted by a conical roof. If the common diameter is 56 m, the height of the cylindrical portion is 6 m and the height of the roof from the ground is 30 m, find the area of the canvas used for the tent.

8. A wooden article as shown in the figure was made from a cylinder by scooping out a hemisphere from one end and a cone from other end. Find the total surface area of the article.

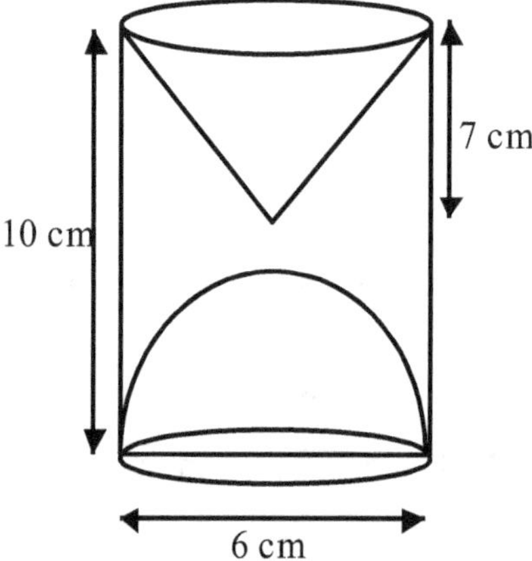

9. A toy is in the form of a cone of radius 3.5 cm surmounted on a hemisphere of same radius. The total height of the toy is 5.6 cm. Find the total surface area of the toy. (Use $\pi = \frac{22}{7}$)

10. A solid is composed of a cylinder with hemispherical ends. If the whole length of the solid is 108 cm and the diameter of the hemispherical ends is 36 cm, find the cost of polishing its surface at the rate of 70 paisa per square cm.

11. A conical tent is made of tarpaulin 1.5 m wide. If the vertical height of the conical tent is 4 m and the base diameter is 6 m; find the length of the tarpaulin used, assuming that 10% extra material is required for wastage due to cutting and stitching margins. (Use $\pi = 3.14$)

12. The largest sphere is carved out of a cube of side 7 cm. Find the volume of sphere.

13. The external length, breadth and height of a closed rectangular wooden box are 18 cm, 10 cm and 6 cm respectively and thickness of wood is $\frac{1}{2}$ cm. When box is empty, it weighs 15 kg and when filled with sand, weighs 100 kg. Find the weighs of 1 cm^3 of wood and sand.

14. It costs Rs. 2200 to paint the inner curved surface of a cylindrical vessel 10 m deep. It the cost of painting is at the rate of Rs. 20/m^2, find the volume of the vessel.

15. Water running in a cylindrical pipe of inner diameter 7 cm is collected in a container at the rate of 192.5 liters per minute. Find the rate of flow of water in the pipe in km/h. (Use $\pi = \frac{22}{7}$)

16. Solid spheres of diameters 6 cm are dropped into a cylindrical beaker containing some water and are fully submerged. If the diameter of the beaker is 18 cm and the water rises by 40 cm in the beaker, find the number of solid spheres dropper in the water.

17. A cubical block of side 7 cm is surmounted by a hemisphere. What is the greatest diameter the hemisphere can have? Find the surface area of the solid.

18. A right circular cylinder having diameter 12 cm and height 15 cm is full of ice cream. The ice cream is to be filled in identical cones of height 12 cm and diameter 6 cm having a hemi spherical shape on the top. Find the number of cones required.

19. The given block is made of two solids: a cone and a hemisphere. If the height and the base – radius of the cone are 24 cm and 10 cm respectively and the diameter of the hemisphere is 10 cm; find the total surface area of the block. (Use $\pi = 3.14$)

20. The radii of the base of two right circular solid cones of same height are r_1 and r_2 respectively. The cones are melted and recast into a solid sphere of radius R. Show that the height of each cone is given by:

$$h = \frac{4R^3}{r_1^2 + r_2^2}$$

$$\boxed{\textbf{ANSWERS}}$$

Short Questions for one or two marks	
Answer 1.	d
Answer 2.	d
Answer 3.	b
Answer 4.	d
Answer 5.	c
Answer 6.	b
Answer 7.	b
Answer 8.	a
Answer 9.	b
Answer 10.	a
Answer 11.	d
Answer 12.	12 cm
Answer 13.	3150 cm^2
Answer 14.	572 cm^2
Answer 15.	7 cm
Three and four marks questions	
Answer 1.	45
Answer 2.	4
Answer 3.	210 cm^2, 200 cm^3
Answer 4.	10.8% approx.
Answer 5.	(i) 7m (ii) 24m (iii) 275m
Answer 6.	246.4 cm^3
Answer 7.	$\left(1056 + 352\sqrt{85}\right)$ m
Answer 8.	$\left(78 + 3\sqrt{58}\right)\pi \text{ cm}^2$

Answer 9.	214.5 cm^2
Answer 10.	Rs. 8553.60
Answer 11.	34.54 m
Answer 12.	$\dfrac{539}{3} \text{ cm}^3$
Answer 13.	$1 \text{ cm}^3 \text{ Wood} = \dfrac{1}{21} \text{ kg}, 1 \text{ cm}^3 \text{ of sand} = \dfrac{85}{765} \text{ kg}$
Answer 14.	$\dfrac{385}{4} \text{ m}^3$
Answer 15.	3 km/h
Answer 16.	90
Answer 17.	7 cm, 332.5 cm^2
Answer 18.	10
Answer 19.	1208.9 cm^2

Statistics

Introduction: The basic idea of statistics is the extraction of meaningful information from raw data. Statistics deals with collection, organization, analysis and interpretation of data.

1.1 Measure of central tendency: A statistical data represented by some numerical expressions, called **Measures of Central Tendency** or **averages.** A certain value representing a set of data values. It indicates where most values in a distribution fall. Out of many types of statistical averages, only three averages will be studied here:

(i) Arithmetic Mean (or simply Mean)
(ii) Median
(iii) Mode

Remark:

1. For calculation of any Measures of Central Tendency **class intervals** should be **continuous**. If they are not continuous, make them continuous first using **adjustment factor**. Here is an example for this:

$$\text{Adjustment factor} = \frac{\text{Lower limit of a class} - \text{Upper limit of previous class}}{2}$$

Now rewrite class intervals by (lower limit – adjustment factor) and (upper limit + adjustment factor).

For example:

Marks	11-20	21-30	31-40	41-50	51-60	61-70	71-80
No. of students	2	6	10	12	9	7	4

Solution: Here class intervals are discontinuous, so adjustment factor $= \frac{21-20}{2} = 0.5$

Marks (before adjustment)	Marks (after adjustment)
$11 - 20$	$10.5 - 20.5$
$21 - 30$	$20.5 - 30.5$
$31 - 40$	$30.5 - 40.5$
$41 - 50$	$40.5 - 50.5$
$51 - 60$	$50.5 - 60.5$
$61 - 70$	$60.5 - 70.5$
$71 - 80$	$70.5 - 80.5$

2. Class mark: For each class interval, we require a point which would serve as the representative of the whole class. It is assumed that the frequency of each class interval is centered around its midpoint, called **class mark**.

$$\text{Class Marks} = \frac{\text{upper class limit+lower class limit}}{2}$$

$$\boxed{\textbf{Arithmetic Mean}}$$

1.1 Arithmetic mean: Arithmetic mean (mean) is the sum of a collection of data divided by the sum of the data.

For Example:

The mean of n numbers $x_1, x_2, x_3 \ldots \ldots \ldots, x_n$ is $= \dfrac{x_1+x_2+x_3+\ldots\ldots\ldots\ldots+x_n}{n} = \dfrac{\Sigma x}{n}$

The Greek later Σ (Sigma) means sum of number. This method is used when data is ungrouped (Non tabular).

1.2 Arithmetic mean of Tabulated (grouped data): The arithmetic mean can be obtained by using any one of the following three methods:

(i) Direct method

(ii) Short cut Method (assumed mean method)

(iii) Step – deviation-method

1.3 Direct Method: Mean using direct method: Mean $= \dfrac{\Sigma f x}{\Sigma f}$

Steps:

1. Find the class mark (x) of each class (if not given already).

$$\text{Class mark} = \dfrac{\text{Lower limit} + \text{Upper limit}}{2}$$

2. Calculate fx for each x.
3. Find Σfx and Σf.
4. Use the formula to calculate the mean.

Example: Find mean of the following data using direct method.

Class interval	20 - 30	30 – 40	40 – 50	50 – 60	60 - 70	70 - 80
Frequency	10	6	8	12	5	9

Solution:

Class interval	Class mark (x)	Frequency (f)	fx
20 – 30	25	10	250
30 – 40	35	6	210
40 – 50	45	8	360
50 – 60	55	12	660
60 – 70	65	5	325
70 – 80	75	9	675
	$\Sigma f = 50$		$\Sigma fx = 2480$

$$\text{Mean} = \dfrac{\Sigma fx}{\Sigma f}$$
$$= \dfrac{2480}{50}$$
$$= 49.6 \textbf{ Ans.}$$

1.4 Short – cut Method (Assumed mean method): Mean using short – cut method:

$$\text{Mean} = A + \frac{\Sigma \, fd}{\Sigma \, f}$$

Steps:

1. Find the class mark (x) of each class (if not given already).

$$\text{Class mark} = \frac{\text{Lower limit} + \text{Upper limit}}{2}$$

2. Choose a suitable number from the middle of class mark (x) column, known as assumed mean (A)
3. Calculate the deviation (d) of each x from assumed mean i.e. $d = x - A$
4. Calculate fd for each x.
5. Find Σfd and Σf.
6. Use the formula to calculate the mean.

Example: Find mean of the table given in **section 1.3** using short cut method.

Solution:

Class interval	Class mark (x)	Frequency (f)	Deviation (d) $d = (x - A)$	fd
$20 - 30$	25	10	-30	-300
$30 - 40$	35	6	-20	-120
$40 - 50$	45	8	-10	-80
$50 - 60$	$55 = A$	12	0	0
$60 - 70$	65	5	10	50
$70 - 80$	75	9	20	180
	$\Sigma f = 50$			$\Sigma fd = -270$

$$\text{Mean} = A + \frac{\Sigma \, fd}{\Sigma \, f}$$

$$= 55 + \left(\frac{-270}{50}\right)$$

$$= 49.6 \quad \textbf{Ans.}$$

Remark: If each observation of mean is updated by a quantity say x, then mean is also updated by the same quantity.

For example:

1. If a number say x is added or subtracted from each observation, then their mean is also increased or decreased by x.

   If $\bar{x}$ is is mean of $a_1, a_2, a_3, \ldots, a_n$, then mean of $(a_1 \pm x), (a_2 \pm x), (a_3 \pm x), \ldots (a_n \pm x)$ will be $\bar{x} \pm x$.

2. If a number say x is multiplied with each observation, then their mean is also multiplied by x.

   If $\bar{x}$ is is mean of $a_1, a_2, a_3, \ldots, a_n$, then mean of $(a_1 \times x), (a_2 \times x), (a_3 \times x), \ldots (a_n \times x)$ will be $\bar{x} * x$.

3. If each observation is divided by a quantity say x, then their mean is also divide by x.

   If $\bar{x}$ is is mean of $a_1, a_2, a_3, \ldots, a_n$, then mean of $\frac{a_1}{x}, \frac{a_2}{x}, \frac{a_3}{x}, \ldots, \frac{a_n}{x}$ will be $\frac{\bar{x}}{x}$.

Practice Sheet - 1

(Based on Mean)

Short questions for one or two marks:

1. The mean of 5 observations $x, x + 2, x + 4, x + 6$ and $x + 8$ is 11, then the value of x is:

    (a) 4   (b) 7   (c) 11   (d) 6

2. The mean of 20 numbers is 13. The new mean if each observation is increased by 5, is:

    (a) 13   (b) 18   (c) 65   (d) 8

3. If the mean of 4, 5, a, 6, b, 9 and 11 is 10, then find the value of (a + b).

    (a) 35   (b) 34   (c) 53   (d) 33

4. Find the arithmetic mean of 1, 2, 3, 4, 5, ... , n.

5. Calculate the arithmetic mean of first five prime numbers.

6. Find the mean of the following distribution.

X	4	6	9	10	15
F	5	10	10	7	8

7. Find the value of p, if the mean of the following distribution is 7.5.

X	3	5	7	9	11	13
F	6	8	15	p	8	4

Three and four marks questions:

1. Find the mean of the following distribution using
(i) Direct method
(ii) Short cut method

Class	$0-10$	$10-20$	$20-30$	$30-40$	40 - 50
Frequency	12	16	6	7	9

2. The following are the marks obtained by 100 students in a class test.

Marks	$0-10$	10 - 20	$20-30$	$30-40$	$40-50$	$50-60$
No. of students	12	18	27	20	17	6

    Calculate the mean marks by Short cut method

3. Calculate the mean of the distribution, given below, using the short cut method:

Marks	11-20	21-30	31-40	41-50	51-60	61-70	71-80
No. of students	2	6	10	12	9	7	4

4. The arithmetic mean of the following distribution is 25. Determine the value of p.

Class	$0-10$	10 - 20	$20-30$	30 - 40	40 - 50
Frequency	5	18	15	p	6

5. The marks obtained by 120 students in mathematics test is given in the following distribution.

Marks	$0-20$	20 - 40	$40-60$	$60-80$	$80-100$	Total
No. of students	17	f_1	32	f_2	19	120

The mean of the following distribution is 50 and the sum of the frequencies is 120. Find the missing frequencies f_1 and f_2.

6. Find the value of p, if the mean of the following distribution is 20.

x	15	17	19	$20 + p$	23
f	2	3	4	$5p$	6

7. The mean of the following data is 16. Calculate the value of f.

Marks	5	10	15	20	25
No. of Students	3	7	f	9	6

8. The data on the number of patients attending a hospital in the morning are given below. Find the average (mean) number of patients attending the hospital in a month by using the shortcut method.

No. of patients	10 – 20	20 - 30	30 – 40	40 – 50	50 – 60	60 – 70
No. of days	5	2	7	9	2	5

Take the assumed mean as 45. Give your answer correct to 2 decimal places.

9. Find the mean of first five even natural numbers. If x denotes each even natural number, and their mean is $\bar{x}$, then show that $\Sigma(x - \bar{x}) = 0$.

ANSWERS

Short Questions for one or two marks	
Answer 1.	b
Answer 2.	b
Answer 3.	a
Answer 4.	$\dfrac{(n + 1)}{2}$
Answer 5.	5
Answer 6.	9
Answer 7.	$p = 3$

Three and four marks questions	
Answer 1.	22
Answer 2.	28
Answer 3.	46.9
Answer 4.	$p = 16$
Answer 5.	$f_1 = 28, f_2 = 24$
Answer 6.	$p = 1$
Answer 7.	$f = 15$
Answer 8.	40.33
Answer 9.	mean = 6

$$\boxed{\textbf{Median}}$$

Introduction: Median is the value of **middle** most observation of the **arranged** data either in ascending or descending order. Median divides the arranged series into two equal parts i.e, 50% of the observation lie below the median and the remaining are above the median.

1.5 Median for raw data:

Steps:

1. First arrange the data in ascending or descending order.

2. Find n (number of observations).

3. If n is odd then median $= \left(\dfrac{n+1}{2}\right)^{th}$ term.

If n is even then median $= \dfrac{\left(\dfrac{n}{2}\right)^{th} \text{term} + \left(\dfrac{n}{2}+1\right)^{th} \text{term}}{2}$

1.6 Median for tabulated data (When class intervals are not given):

Steps:

1. First construct a cumulating frequency distribution table.

2. Find n (sum of all frequencies). If n is **odd** then from the cumulative frequencies find the value just greater than or equal to $\left(\dfrac{n+1}{2}\right)$ and take the corresponding value from **class mark (x)**. This is the required **median**.

3. If n is **even** then from the cumulating frequencies find the value just greater than or equal to $\dfrac{n}{2}$ and $\dfrac{n}{2}+1$, and take the corresponding values from **class marks (x)**. The mean of these observations is the required median.

1.7 Median of a grouped frequency distribution:

Steps:

1. Prepare a cumulative frequency distribution table from the given frequency distribution.

(Cumulative frequency defined as a consecutive sum of frequencies. Cumulative frequency distribution is of two types: less than type and more than type. Which is discussed in section 1.9. The frequency distribution is the given below example is of less than type)

2. Find n (sum of frequencies) and calculate $\dfrac{n}{2}$.

3. From the cumulative frequency column find the cumulative frequency just greater than or equal to $\dfrac{n}{2}$, and mark the class interval against that cumulative frequency as **median class**.

4. Calculation the median, by using the given formula:

$$\text{Median} = l + \left(\dfrac{\frac{n}{2}-cf}{f}\right) \times h$$

Where l = lower limit of median class

    cf = cumulative frequency of the class preceding the median class

    f = frequency of the median class

    h = class size

Example:

Find the median of the following data:

Class intervals	0 – 10	10 – 20	20 – 30	30 – 40	40 – 50
Frequency	5	25	25	18	7

Step 1: Prepare a cumulative frequency (cf) distribution table:

Class intervals	Frequency	Cumulative frequency
0 – 10	5	5
10 – 20	25	$5 + 25 = 30$
20 – 30	25	$5 + 25 + 25 = 55$
30 – 40	18	$5 + 25 + 25 + 18 = 73$
40 – 50	7	$5 + 25 + 25 + 18 + 7 = 80$
Total	$n = 80$	

Step 2: Find $\dfrac{n}{2}$; i.e. $\dfrac{80}{2} = 40$ here

Step 3: From cumulative frequency column 55 is just greater than 40, so **median class is 20 – 30**.

Step 4: From the formula Median $= l + \left(\dfrac{\frac{n}{2} - cf}{f}\right) \times$ h

$$\text{Where} \quad l = 20$$
$$cf = 30$$
$$f = 25$$
$$h = 10$$

$$\text{Median} = 20 + \left(\frac{\frac{80}{2} - 30}{25}\right) \times 10$$

$$= 20 + \left(\frac{40 - 30}{25}\right) \times 10$$

$$= 20 + \left(\frac{10}{25}\right) \times 10$$

$$= 20 + 4$$

$$= 24 \quad \textbf{Ans.}$$

1.8 Cumulative frequency distribution: Less than type

Marks	0 – 10	10 – 20	20 – 30	30 – 40	40 – 50
No. of students	5	25	25	18	7

No. of students who has scored marks less than 10 are 5, then the number of students who has scored marks less than 20 include those students also who have scored marks between 0 – 10. So the total number of students with marks less than 20 are $5 + 25 = 30$ and so on.

Marks obtained	Number of students (Cumulative frequency)
Less than 10	5
Less than 20	$5 + 25 = 30$

Less than 30	$5 + 25 + 25 = 55$
Less than 40	$5 + 25 + 25 + 18 = 73$
Less than 50	$5 + 25 + 25 + 18 + 7 = 80$

Remark: In the above table 10, 20, 30, 40 and 50 are the upper limits of the respective class intervals.

1.9 Cumulative frequency distribution: More than type

Marks	$0 - 10$	$10 - 20$	$20 - 30$	$30 - 40$	$40 - 50$
No. of students	5	25	25	18	7

In more than type distribution, we make the table for the number of students who scored more than 0 (i.e., all) are 80, then the number of students who scored more than 10 exclude those students who scored more than 0 $= 80 - 5 = 75$ and so on.

Marks obtained	Number of students (Cumulative frequency)
More than 0	80
More than 10	$80 - 5 = 75$
More than 20	$75 - 25 = 50$
More than 30	$50 - 25 = 25$
More than 40	$25 - 18 = 7$

Remark: In the above table 0, 10, 20, 30 and 40 are the lower limits of the respective class intervals.

Practice Sheet - 2

(Based on Median)

Short questions for one or two Marks:

1. The middle most observation of a statistical data has value which is called:

    (a) Mean   (b) Median   (c) Mode   (d) None of these

2. A data has 25 observations arranged in descending order. Which observation represents the median?

    (a) 12th   (b) 13th   (c) 14th   (d) 15th

3. Find the median of 7, 18, 11, 14, 28, 21 and 24.

4. If the median of the data $6, 7, x - 2, x, 17, 20$ written in ascending order, is 16. Then the value of x:

    (a) 15   (b) 16   (c) 17   (d) 18

5. If 35 is removed from the data: 30, 34, 35, 36, 37, 38, 39, 40, then the median increases by:

    (a) 2   (b) 1.5   (c) 1   (d) 0.5

6. The weight of 45 children in a class were recorded, to the nearest kg, as follows:

Wt. (in nearest kg)	46	48	50	52	5	54	55
No. of children	7	5	8	12	10	2	1

Calculate the median weight.

7. Write the median class of the following distribution. Calculate median also.

Class intervals	$0-10$	$10-20$	$20-30$	$30-40$	$40-50$	$50-60$	$60-70$
Frequency	4	4	8	10	12	8	4

8. Construct the frequency distribution table for the given data.

Marks	Less than 10	Less than 20	Less than 30	Less than 40	Less than 50	Less than 60
No. of students	14	22	37	58	67	75

9. Find the median

Marks obtained	20	25	35	40	50
No. of Students	5	11	24	16	5

Three and four marks questions:

1. Find the median of the following data:

Marks	$0-10$	$10-20$	$20-30$	$30-40$	$40-50$	Total
No. of students	8	16	36	34	6	100

2. If the median of the following frequency distribution is 27.5, then .Find the missing frequencies.

Class intervals	$0-10$	$10-20$	$20-30$	$30-40$	$40-50$	$50-60$	Total
Frequency	3	f_1	20	15	f_2	5	60

3. Find the median wage in the following table.

Wages	0-10	10-20	20-30	30-40	40-50	50-60	60-70	70-80
No. of workers	12	20	30	38	24	16	12	8

4. Find the median of the following data:

Profit (in lakhs of rupees)	Number of shops
More than or equal to 5	30
More than or equal to 10	28
More than or equal to 15	16
More than or equal to 20	14
More than or equal to 25	10
More than or equal to 30	7
More than or equal to 35	3

5. Given below is a cumulative frequency distribution showing the marks secured by 50 students in a class.

Marks	Below 20	Below 40	Below 60	Below 80	Below 100
Number of students	17	22	29	37	50

Find the median marks.

6. Calculate the median for the following data:

Age (in years)	$19-25$	$26-32$	$33-39$	$40-46$	$47-53$	$54-60$
Frequency	35	96	68	102	35	4

$$\boxed{\textbf{ANSWERS}}$$

Short questions for one or two marks	
Answer 1.	b
Answer 2.	b
Answer 3.	18
Answer 4.	c
Answer 5.	d
Answer 6.	52 kg
Answer 7.	30 – 40
Answer 9.	35
Three and four marks questions	
Answer 1.	27.3
Answer 2.	$f_1 = 10,\ f_2 = 5$
Answer 3.	Rs. 34.74
Answer 4.	17.5
Answer 5.	48.57
Answer 6.	36.51

$$\boxed{\textbf{Mode}}$$

Introduction: The data which appears most often in a set of data is called mode. Or number which has highest frequency is mode. Suppose there are 25 girls and 20 boys in a class, then **mode = girls**. A given data may have the same maximum frequency for more than one observation, then given data is **multimodal (Not in course)**.

1.10 Mode for raw data:

Example: Calculate the mean, the median and the mode of the following numbers: 3, 1, 5, 6, 3, 4, 5, 3, 7, 2.

Solution: In the given set of numbers 3 occurs most frequently, so mode = 3

1.11 Mode for tabulated data (without class intervals):

Example: In a class of 40 students, marks obtained by the students in a class test (out of 10) are given below:

Marks	1	2	3	4	5	6	7	8	9	10
Number of students	1	2	3	3	6	10	5	4	3	3

Calculate mode for the given distribution:

Solution: In the given distribution variate 6 has the highest frequency i.e. 10 so mode in 6.

1.12. Mode for grouped data:

In a grouped frequency distribution, it is not possible to determine the mode by looking at the frequencies. Here we can only locate a class with the maximum frequency, called the **modal class**. The mode is a value within the modal class, and determines using the given formula:

$$\text{Mode} = l + \left(\frac{f_1 - f_0}{2f_1 - f_0 - f_2}\right) \times h$$

Where l = lower limit of the modal class.

h = size of the class interval (assuming all class sizes are equal).

f_1 = frequency of the modal class.

f_0 = frequency of the class preceding the modal class.

f_2 = frequency of the class succeeding he modal class.

Example: Find the mode of the following data:

Class intervals	20 – 30	30 – 40	40 – 50	50 – 60	60 – 70
Frequency	12	10	25	15	8

Solution:

Step 1: Observe the highest frequency and locate the modal class.

Here the highest frequency is 25, so modal class is 40 – 50. So $l = 40$

Step 2: Find the values of f_0, f_1, f_2 and h. Since the modal class is 40 – 50

So, Frequency of modal class $(f_1) = 25$

Frequency of class preceding the modal class $(f_0) = 10$

Frequency of class succeeding the modal class $(f_2) = 15$

Class height $(h) = 20 - 30 = 10$

Step 3: substitute these values in the given formula and find mode.

$$\text{Mode} = l + \left(\frac{f_1 - f_0}{2f_1 - f_0 - f_2}\right) \times h$$

$$\text{Mode} = 40 + \left(\frac{25 - 10}{2 \times 25 - 10 - 15}\right) \times 10$$

$$\text{Mode} = 40 + \left(\frac{15}{25}\right) \times 10$$

$$\text{Mode} = 40 + 6 = 46 \qquad \textbf{Ans.}$$

1.13 Empirical relationship: In statistics there is a relation between mean, median and mode, called Empirical relationship.

$$\textbf{3 Median = Mode + 2 Mean}$$

Practice Sheet - 3

(Based on Mode)

Short questions for one or two marks:

1. Mode is:
(a) Least frequent value   (b) Middle most value
(c) Most frequent value   (d) None of these

2. If the mode of the data $64, 60, 48, x, 43, 48, 43, 34$ *is* 43, then $x + 3 =$

   (a) 44   (b) 45   (c) 46   (d) 48

3. Find the modal class of the following distribution:

Class intervals	$10-20$	$20-30$	$30-40$	$40-50$	$50-60$
Frequency	12	10	25	15	8

4. Find the mode of the following data:

   2, 3, 5, 1, 3, 2, 4, 2, 3, 2, 6, 0, 2, 2, 5, 3, 4

5. Find the mode for the following frequency distribution:

Marks obtained	0	2	3	4	6	7	9	10
No. of students	3	5	12	18	21	8	2	1

6. Write the relationship connecting three measures of central tendencies. Hence find the mode of the given data if median is 24.5 and mean is 29.75.

Three and four marks questions:

1. For the following data, find mode:

Class intervals	$1-3$	$3-5$	$5-7$	$7-9$	$9-11$
Frequency	14	16	4	4	2

2. If the mode of the following frequency distribution is 31, then find the value of p.

Class	5 – 15	15 – 25	25 – 35	35 – 45	45 – 55
Frequency	3	p	15	11	6

3. The following distribution shows the height of students of a certain class in a certain city:

Height (in cm)	160 – 162	163 – 165	166 – 168	169 – 171	172 – 174
No. of students	15	118	142	127	18

Find the modal height of students:

4. The mode of the following distribution is 65. Find the value of x and y, if sum of the frequency is 50.

Class intervals	0 – 20	20 – 40	40 – 60	60 – 80	80 – 100	100 – 120	120 – 140
Frequency	6	8	x	12	6	y	3

ANSWERS

Short questions for one or two marks	
Answer 1.	c
Answer 2.	c
Answer 3.	30 – 40
Answer 4.	2
Answer 5.	6
Answer 6.	14

Three and four marks questions	
Answer 1.	3.3 (approx.)
Answer 2.	p = 9
Answer 3.	167.35 cm
Answer 4.	$x = 10, y = 5$

Solved
Question Papers

Solved Model Test Paper – 1

Class – X : Session – 2021 – 22

(MATHEMATICS) – Term 2

Time Allowed: 2 hour   **Maximum Marks: 40**

General Instructions:
1. The question paper consists of 14 questions divided into 3 sections A, B, C.
2. All questions are compulsory.
3. Section A comprises of 6 questions of 2 marks each. No internal choice in this section.
4. Section B comprises of 4 questions of 3 marks each. No internal choice in this section.
5. Section C comprises of 4 questions of 4 marks each. It contains two case study based questions. Attempt any four questions from each case study.

Section A

Q. No.   **Marks**

1   If the tangents from an external point are inclined at an angle of 70°, then find the angle   **2**
between the radii drawn through their points of contact.

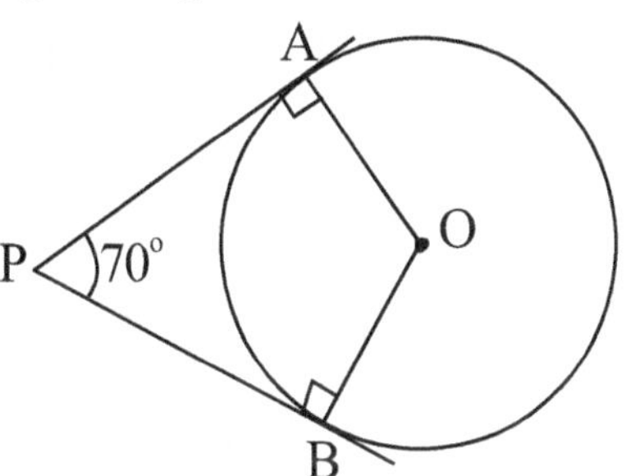

Solution:

In the given figure, $\angle APB = 70^o$ and PA and PB are tangents from P on circle, whose centre is O.

We have to find $\angle AOB$.

We know that tangent makes 90° with the radius at point of contact (Theorem).

So $\angle PAO = \angle PBO = 90^o$

In quadrilateral AOBP,

$\Rightarrow 90^o + 90^o + 70^o + \angle AOB = 360^o$ (angle sum property of quadrilateral)

$\Rightarrow \angle AOB = 360^o - 250^o$

$\angle AOB = 110^o$ **Ans.**

2   Find the value of p, if the mean of the following distribution is 20.   **2**

x	15	17	19	$20 + p$	23
f	6	9	12	$15p$	18

x	f	fx
15	6	90
17	9	153
19	12	228
20+p	15p	300p+15p^2
23	18	414
	$\Sigma f = 45 + 15p$	$\Sigma fx = 15p^2 + 300p + 885$

$$mean = \frac{\Sigma fx}{\Sigma f}$$

$$20 = \frac{15p^2 + 300p + 885}{45 + 15p}$$

$$15p^2 + 300p + 885 = 900 + 300p$$

$$15p^2 = 15$$

$$p = \pm 1$$

But frequency cannot be negative

$$p = 1 \qquad \textbf{Ans.}$$

3 In a right triangle ABC, right angled at B, BC = 15 cm, and AB = 8 cm. A circle is inscribed in triangle ABC. Then find radius of the circle. **2**

Solution:

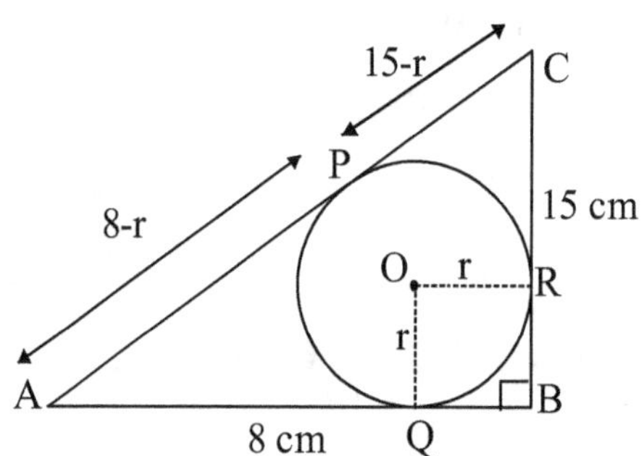

In the given triangle ABC, AB = 8 cm and BC = 15 cm

$$AC = \sqrt{AB^2 + BC^2} \qquad \text{(Pythagoras theorem)}$$

$$AC = \sqrt{8^2 + 15^2}$$

$$AC = \sqrt{289} = 17 \text{ cm}$$

Join OQ and OR, where Q and R are point of contact of tangent AB and BC respectively.

$\angle OQB = \angle ORB = 90°$ (radius makes 90° with tangent at point of contact)

and BQ = BR   (tangent from external point to circle are equal)

So $OQBR$ is a square.

So, $OQ = OR = BQ = BR$ (let r)

$AQ = 8 - r\ cm\ and\ CR = 15 - r\ cm,$

$AP = AQ, and\ CP = CR$ (tangents from external point are equal)

$$AP + PC = AC$$
$$8 - r + 15 - r = 17$$
$$-2r = 17 - 23 = -6$$
$$r = 3 \ cm.$$

radius of circle $= 3 \ cm.$ **Ans.**

4. If 21, a, b, –3 are in A.P., find the value of a + b.   2

Solution:

Since all these terms are in A.P., so common difference is:

$$a - 21 = b - a = -3 - b$$
$$so, a - 21 = -3 - b$$
$$a + b = -3 + 21$$
$$a + b = 18$$ **Ans.**

5. A tangent PA is drawn from an external point P to a circle of radius $3\sqrt{2}$ cm such that the distance of the point P from O is 6 cm as shown in the figure. The value of $\angle APO$.   2

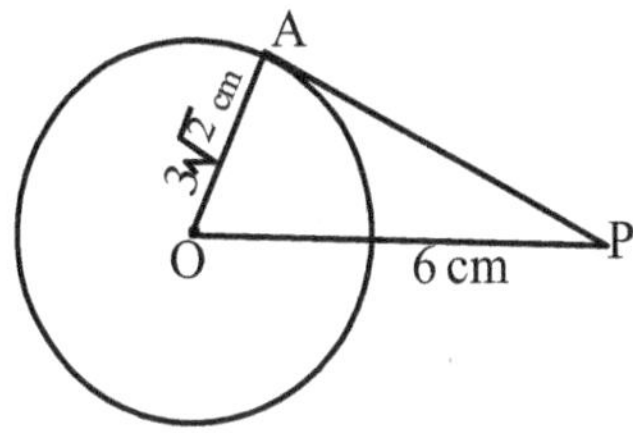

Solutions:

In the following figure, $\angle OAP = 90°$ (radius is perpendicular to tangent at point of contact)

$$\sin \angle AOP = \frac{AO}{PO} \qquad \left(\sin \theta = \frac{perpendicular}{hypotenuse} \right)$$

$$\sin \angle APO = \frac{3\sqrt{2}}{6}$$

$$\sin \angle APO = \frac{\sqrt{2}}{2} \times \frac{\sqrt{2}}{\sqrt{2}}$$

$$\sin \angle APO = \frac{2}{2\sqrt{2}}$$

$$\sin \angle APO = \frac{1}{\sqrt{2}}, \text{ but we know that } \sin 45° = \frac{1}{\sqrt{2}}$$

So $\angle APO = 45^o$ **Ans.**

6. State the modal class and find the mode of the following distribution.   2

Height (in cm)	30-40	40-50	50-60	60-70	70-80	80-90
No of plants	4	3	8	11	6	2

Solution:

Modal class is the class with highest frequency, so modal class is $60 - 70$

Lower limit (l) of modal class $h = 60$, class size $= 10$

Frequency (f_1) of the modal class = 11, frequency (f_0) of class preceding the modal class = 8

Frequency (f_2) of class succeeding the modal class = 6

$$\text{Mode} = l + \left(\frac{f_1 - f_0}{2f_1 - f_0 - f_2}\right) \times h$$

$$= 60 + \left(\frac{11 - 8}{22 - 8 - 2}\right) \times 10$$

$$= 60 + \left(\frac{3}{12}\right) \times 10$$

$$= 62.5 \qquad \textbf{Ans.}$$

Section B

7   If roots of a quadratic equation $(b - c)x^2 + (c - a)x + (a - b) = 0$ are real and equal, then prove that $2b = a + c$.   **3**

Solution:

Since roots are equal so discriminant

$$b^2 - 4ac = 0$$
$$(c - a)^2 - 4(b - c)(a - b) = 0$$
$$c^2 - 2ca + a^2 - 4(ba - b^2 - ca + cb) = 0$$
$$c^2 - 2ca + a^2 - 4ba + 4b^2 + 4ca - 4cb = 0$$
$$c^2 + 2ca + a^2 - 4ba + 4b^2 - 4cb = 0$$
$$a^2 + 4b^2 + c^2 + 2ca - 4ba - 4cb = 0$$
$$a^2 + (-2b)^2 + c^2 + 2ca - 4ba - 4cb = 0$$
$$(a - 2b + c)^2 = 0 \qquad [(a + b + c)^2 = a^2 + b^2 + c^2 + 2ab + 2bc + 2ac]$$
$$a - 2b + c = 0$$
$$a + c = 2b$$

Hence Proved.

8   Solve using factorization method: $\sqrt{3}x^2 + 10x + 7\sqrt{3} = 0$ **3**

Solution:

$$\sqrt{3}x^2 + 10x + 7\sqrt{3} = 0$$

$$\sqrt{3}x^2 + 7x + 3x + 7\sqrt{3} = 0$$

$$x(\sqrt{3}x + 7) + \sqrt{3}(\sqrt{3}x + 7) = 0$$

$$(\sqrt{3}x + 7)(x + \sqrt{3}) = 0$$

Apply zero product rule:

$$x = -\sqrt{3}, \frac{-7}{\sqrt{3}} \qquad \textbf{Ans.}$$

9   Draw two tangents to a circle of radius 3.5 cm from a point P at a distance of 6.2 cm from its centre.   **3**

Solution:

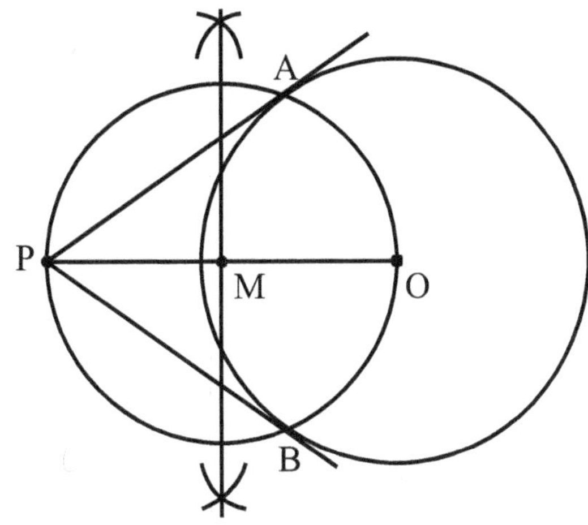

1. Draw a circle of radius 3.5 cm with centre O.
2. Take a point P outside the circle so that OP = 6.2 cm
3. Take OP as diameter. Draw perpendicular bisector of OP.
4. OM as radius and M as centre draw a circle which intersect the first circle at two point A and B.
5. Join PA and PB. These two are the required tangents.

10 A kite is flying, attached to a thread which is 165 m long. The thread makes an angle of 30° with the ground. Find the height of the kite from the ground, assuming that there is no slack in the thread. **3**

Solution:

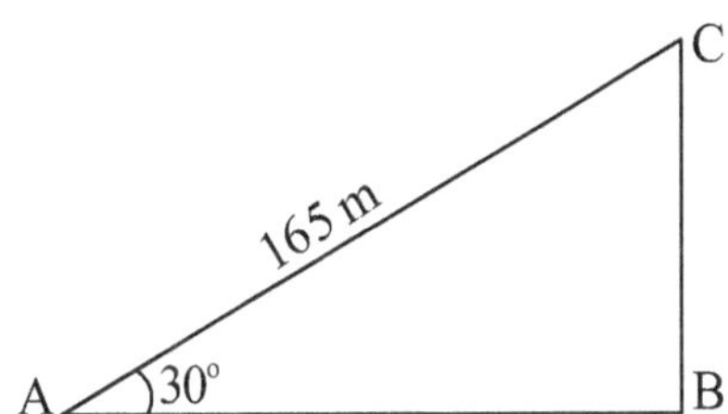

From the given figure C is the Kite, AC = 165 m is the thread and angle BAC = 30°

$$\sin 30° = \frac{BC}{AC} \qquad \left(\sin \theta = \frac{\text{perpendicular}}{\text{hypotenuse}}\right)$$

$$\frac{1}{2} = \frac{BC}{165} \Rightarrow BC = \frac{165}{2}$$

BC = 82.5 m

Height of kite from the ground = 82.5 m **Ans.**

Section C

11 Find the median wage in the following table. **4**

Wages	0-10	10-20	20-30	30-40	40-50	50-60	60-70	70-80
No. of workers	12	20	30	38	24	16	12	8

Solution:

From the given distribution, first find cumulative frequency of all class and $\frac{n}{2}$:

wages	No. of workers	cumulative frequency
0 - 10	12	12
10 - 20	20	32
20 - 30	30	62
30 - 40	38	100
40 - 50	24	124
50 - 60	16	140
60 - 70	12	152
70 - 80	8	160
$n = 160$		

In the distribution above $n = 160$, so $\frac{n}{2} = 80$. Now $30 - 40$ is the class whose cumulative frequency 100 is greater than (and nearest) to $\frac{n}{2}$, i.e., 80, so according to formula

$$\text{median} = l + \left(\frac{\frac{n}{2} - cf}{f}\right) \times h$$

lower limit of median class $(l) = 30$

number of observation $(n) = 160$

cumulative frequency of class preceding the median class $(cf) = 62$

frequency of the median class $(f) = 38$

class size (assuming class size to be equal) $(h) = 10$

substituting these values in the formula above

$$\text{median} = 30 + \left(\frac{80-62}{38}\right) \times 10$$

$$\text{median} = 30 + \left(\frac{17}{38}\right) \times 10$$

$$\text{median} = 30 + 4.473$$

$$\text{median} = 34.47 \text{ (approx.)} \qquad \textbf{Ans.}$$

12. In the given figure, ΔABC is drawn to circumscribe a circle of radius 10 cm. Such that the segment BP and CP into which BC is divided by the point of contact P, are of lengths 15 cm and 20 cm respectively. If the area of ΔABC = 525 cm², then find the lengths of sides AB and AC.   **4**

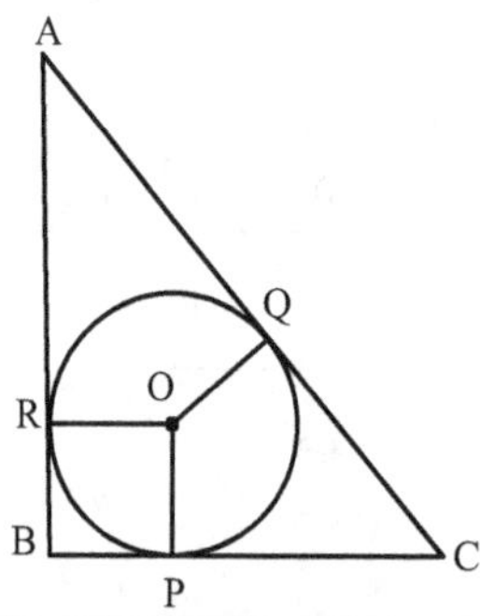

Solution:

Given BP = 15 cm and CP = 20 cm and area of ΔABC = 525 cm^2,

we know that the lengths of tangents drawn from and external point to a circle are equal

so $\qquad BR = BP = 15\ cm$

$\qquad\qquad CQ = CP = 20\ cm$

$\qquad\qquad AQ = AR = x\ cm\ (let)$

Now $\qquad BC = BP + CP$

$\qquad\qquad = 15 + 20 = 35\ cm$

$\qquad AB = AR + BR$

$\qquad\qquad = (x + 15)\ cm$

$\qquad AC = AQ + CQ$

$\qquad\qquad = (x + 20)\ cm$

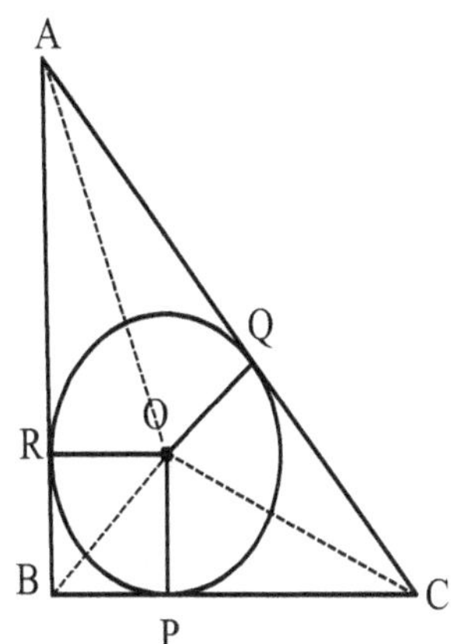

$OP \perp BC, OQ \perp AC$ and $OR \perp AB$

$\because$ (A tangent to a circle is perpendicular to the radius at the point of contact)

Join OA, OB and OC.

Area(ΔABC) = area (Δ OBC) + area (Δ AOC) + area (Δ AOB)

$$525 = \tfrac{1}{2} \times OP \times BC + \tfrac{1}{2} \times OQ \times AC + \tfrac{1}{2} \times OR \times AB$$

$$525 = \tfrac{1}{2} \times 10 \times 35 + \tfrac{1}{2} \times 10 \times (x + 20) + \tfrac{1}{2} \times 10 \times (x + 15)$$

$$525 = 5(35 + x + 20 + x + 15)$$

$$525 = 2x + 70$$

$$2x = 35$$

$$x = 17.5\ cm$$

$$AB = x + 15 = 17.5 + 15$$

$$= 35.5\ cm$$

$$AC = x + 20 = 17.5 + 20$$

$$= 37.5\ cm \qquad\qquad \textbf{Ans.}$$

Case Study based – 1 (Bank Loan)

13

Ravish was wishing to buy a new car but he didnt had enough of money. One of his friend suggested him to take a loan from XYZ bank. Influenced by his idea, he decides to take a loan of Rs. 1,18,000 and decides to repay by Rs. 1000 per month. On a further note, he decides to increase the installment by Rs. 100 every month. Answer the following questions.

(a) What is the amount paid by him in 30th installment?   **1**

    (i)   Rs. 3900

    (ii)   Rs. 3800

    (iii)   Rs. 3700

    (iv)   Rs. 3600

Solution: Option (i) is correct

First term a = 1000 and common difference (d) = 100

$So\ t_{30} = a + 29d = 1000 + 29 \times 100$
$$= Rs.\ 3900$$

(b) What is the total amount paid by him in 30 installments?   **1**

    (i)   Rs. 74000

    (ii)   Rs. 75000

    (iii)   Rs. 73000

    (iv)   Rs. 73500

Solution: Option (iv) is correct

Total amount paid in 30 installment is given by $S_n = \frac{n}{2}(a + l)$

$$S_{30} = \frac{30}{2}(1000 + 3900) \qquad (l = t_{30})$$
$$= 15 \times 4900 = Rs.\ 73500$$

(c) What amount is left after 30th installment?   **1**

    (i)   Rs. 44500

    (ii)   Rs. 45000

    (iii)   Rs. 45500

    (iv)   Rs. 40000

Solution: Option (i) is correct

Till 30th installment Rs. 73500 paid, so remaining balance amount = 118000 − 73500 = Rs. 44500

(d) If the total number of installments is 40, what is the amount paid in the last installment?   **1**

    (i)   Rs. 4900

    (ii)   Rs. 4800

    (iii)   Rs. 4300

    (iv)   Rs. 4500

Solution: Option (i) is correct.

Amount paid in the last installment $t_{40} = a + 39\ d = 1000 + 39 \times 100 = Rs.\ 4900$

(e) What is the ratio of first and last installment?   **1**

    (i)   1 : 49

    (ii)   10 : 49

    (iii)   49 : 1

(iv)   49 : 10

Solution: Option (ii) is correct

Ratio of first and last installment = 1000 : 4900 = 10 : 49.

Case Study based – 2 (Test Tube)

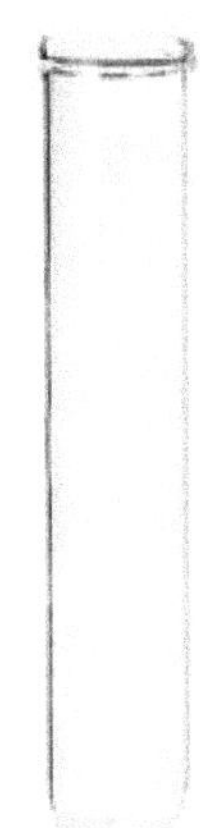

A student performing a test using test tube in a chemistry lab. The test tube is shown in the above figure.

(a) What shapes are found in a test tube?   1

    (i)   Cylinder

    (ii)   Hemi – sphere

    (iii)   Both A and B

    (iv)   None of the above

Solution: Option (iii) is correct.

(b) What is the volume of cylinder when radius is 1 cm and total height is 12 cm? (Take $\pi = 3.14$)   1

    (i)   30 cm^3

    (ii)   31.4 cm^3

    (iii)   33.81 cm^3

    (iv)   35 cm^3

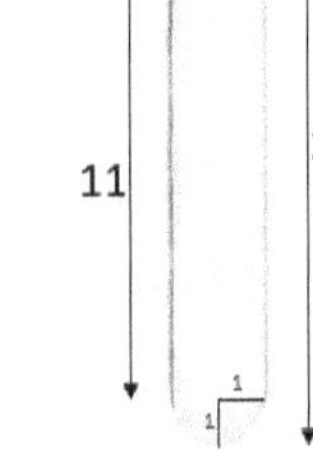

Solution: Option (iv) is correct

Radius $r = 1$ cm, height of cylindrical part $h = 12 - 1 = 11$ cm

volume of cylinder $= \pi r^2 h$

$$= 3.14 \times 1 \times 1 \times 11 = 34.54 \text{ cm}^3. \text{ Nearest value is 35 cm}^3.$$

(c) What is the volume of hemisphere?   1

    (i)   3 cm^3

    (ii)   1.4 cm^3

    (iii)   3.81 cm^3

    (iv)   2.093 cm^3

Solution: Option (iv) is correct

Radius $r = 1$

volume of hamisphare $= \frac{2}{3} \pi r^3 = \frac{2}{3} \times 3.14 \times 1 \times 1 \times 1 = 2.093$ cm^3

(d) What is the total volume?   1

(i)   33 cm^3

(ii)   39.77 cm^3

(iii)   35. 21 cm^3

(iv)   36.4 cm^3

Solution: Option (iv) is correct

Total Volume of vessel = 2.093 + 34.54 = 36.633 cm^3

(e) What is the total volume when two test tubes are placed together which becomes like a tablet?   **1**

(i)   66.986 cm^3

(ii)   66 cm^3

(iii)   72.8 cm^3

(iv)   80 cm^3

Solution: Option (iii) is correct

Volume of two test tube = 2 ×36.633 = 73.266 cm^3 (approx.), Nearest is 72.8 cm^3

Solved Model Test Paper – 2

Class – X : Session – 2021 – 22

(MATHEMATICS) – Term 2

Time Allowed: 2 hour   **Maximum Marks: 40**

General Instructions:
1. The question paper consists of 14 questions divided into 3 sections A, B, C.
2. All questions are compulsory.
3. Section A comprises of 6 questions of 2 marks each.
4. Section B comprises of 4 questions of 3 marks each. No internal choice in this section.
5. Section C comprises of 4 questions of 4 marks each. It contains two case study based questions. Attempt any four questions from each case study.

Section A

Q. No   **Marks**

1   Determine the value of 'k' for which $k^2 + 4k + 8$, $2k^2 + 3k + 6$ and $3k^2 + 4k + 4$ are in A.P.   2

Solution:

Since these terms are in A.P., so their common difference will be same,

$$2k^2 + 3k + 6 - (k^2 + 4k + 8) = 3k^2 + 4k + 4 - (2k^2 + 3k + 6)$$
$$2k^2 + 3k + 6 - k^2 - 4k - 8 = 3k^2 + 4k + 4 - 2k^2 - 3k - 6$$
$$k^2 - k - 2 = k^2 + k - 2$$
$$k = 0 \qquad \textbf{Ans.}$$

2   If the median of the data 6, 7, $x - 2$, x, 17, 20 written in ascending order, is 16. Then find the value of x.   2

Solution:

Here number of observation n = 6 (even)

$$\text{So} = \frac{1}{2}\left[\left(\frac{n}{2}\right)^{th} + \left(\frac{n}{2} + 1\right)^{th}\right]$$

$$32 = x - 2 + x$$
$$2x = 34$$
$$x = 17 \qquad\qquad \textbf{Ans.}$$

3   Solve using factorization method: $5^{x+1} + 5^{2-x} = 5^3 + 1$ 2

Solution:

$$5^x \times 5^1 + 5^2 \times 5^{-x} = 125 + 1$$
$$5^x \times 5 + 25 \times \frac{1}{5^x} = 126$$

Let $5^x = p$

$$\text{So, } 5p + \frac{25}{p} = 126$$

$$\frac{5p^2 + 25}{p} = 126$$

$$5p^2 - 126p + 25 = 0$$

$$5p^2 - 125p - p + 25 = 0$$

$$5p(p - 25) - 1(p - 25) = 0$$

$$(p - 25)(5p - 1) = 0$$

$$p = 25, \frac{1}{5}$$

$$5^x = 25$$

$$5^x = 5^2$$

$$x = 2$$

$$5^x = \frac{1}{5}$$

$$5^x = 5^{-1}$$

$$x = -1 \qquad \textbf{Ans. } x = 2, -1$$

4 Δ ABC is isosceles with AB = AC. A circle touches all sides of the triangle, then prove that   **2**

BQ = QC.

Solution:

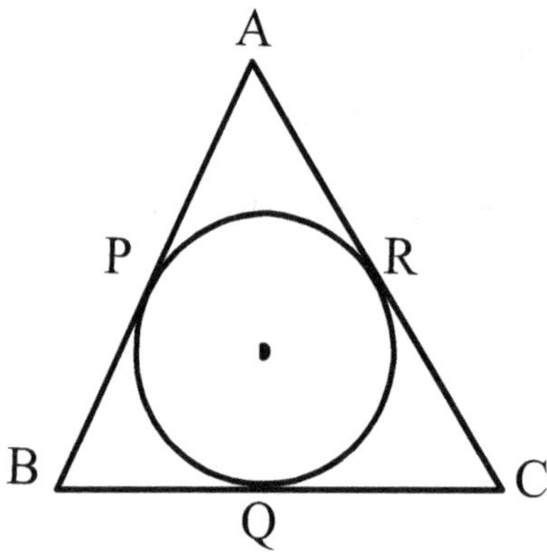

Given, AB = AC

AP + PB = AR + RC

     PB = RC   (AP = AR, as tangents from external point are equal)

     BQ = CQ   (tangents from external point are equal,

           so PB = BQ and RC = CQ)

Hence proved

5   Find the mean of the following distribution using direct method.   **2**

Class	0 – 10	10 – 20	20 – 30	30 – 40	40 – 50
Frequency	12	16	6	7	9

Solution:

class intervals	class marks (x)	frequency (f)	fx
0 - 10	5	12	60
10 - 20	15	16	240
20 - 30	25	6	150
30 - 40	35	7	245
40 - 50	45	9	405
		$\sum f = 50$	$\sum fx = 1100$

Mean in direct method $= \dfrac{\sum fx}{\sum f}$

$$= \dfrac{1100}{50} = 22 \qquad \textbf{Ans.}$$

6 The radius and slant height of a right circular cone are in the ratio of 7: 13 and its curved surface area is 286 cm². Find the radius of the cone. (Take $\pi = \dfrac{22}{7}$). **2**

Solution:

Let radius $r = 7x$ cm and slant height $l = 13x$ cm

Curverd surface area = πrl

$$286 = \dfrac{22}{7} \times 7x \times 13x$$

$$286 = 22 \times x \times 13x$$

$$x^2 = \dfrac{286}{22 \times 13}$$

$$x^2 = 1$$

$$x = 1$$

so radius $r = 7x = 7 \times 1 = 7$ cm $\qquad$ **Ans.**

Section B

7 If the angle of elevation of a cloud from a point 200 m above a lake is 30° and the angle of depression of its reflection in the lake is 60°, then find the height of the cloud above the lake. **3**

Solution:

In the figure, A is a point above the lake surface AF = BD = 200 m. C is the cloud.

We have to find the height of the cloud above the lake i.e. DC.

Let DC = DE = h meter

In triangle ABC, tan BAC $= \dfrac{BC}{BA} \left(\tan \theta = \dfrac{\text{perpendicular}}{\text{base}} \right)$

$$\tan 30° = \dfrac{h - 200}{BA}$$

$$\dfrac{1}{\sqrt{3}} = \dfrac{h - 200}{BA}$$

BA $= \sqrt{3}(\, h - 200)$ ………(i)

In triangle ABE

$$\tan BAE = \frac{BE}{BA}$$

$$\tan 60° = \frac{h + 200}{BA}$$

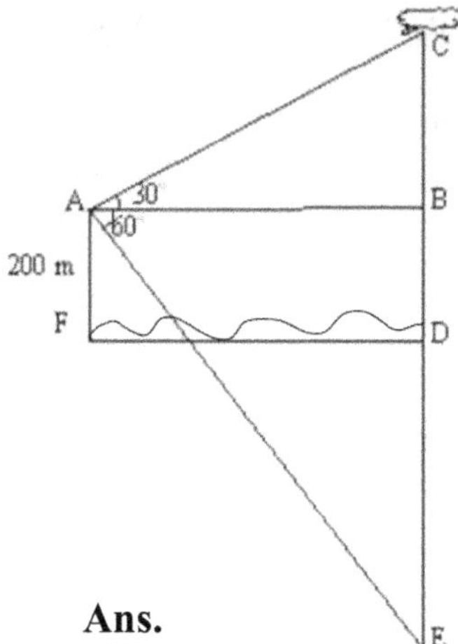

$$\sqrt{3} = \frac{h+200}{\sqrt{3}(h-200)} \text{ (from eq......(i))}$$

$$3h - 600 = h + 200$$

$$2h = 800$$

$$h = 400$$

So height of cloud from water level is 400 m **Ans.**

8 In an A.P., 6th term is half the 4th term, and the 3rd term is 15. How many terms are needed to give a sum that is equal to 66? **3**

Solution:

Let first term be A and common difference is D

$$t_6 = \frac{1}{2}t_4 => 2(A + 5D) = A + 3D$$

$$2A + 10D = A + 3D$$

$$A = -7D \qquad (i)$$

$$t_3 = 15 => A + 2D = 15$$

$$-7D + 2D = 15$$

$$-5D = 15 => D = -3$$

Substitute D in equation (i): $A = -7(-3) = 21$

Let sum of n terms is equal to 66, i.e. $s_n = 66$

$$\frac{n}{2}[2A + (n-1)D] = 66$$

$$n[2 \times 21 + (n-1)(-3)] = 132$$

$$n[42 - 3n + 3] = 132$$

$$n[-3n + 45] - 132 = 0$$

$$-3n^2 + 45n - 132 = 0$$

$$n^2 - 15n + 44 = 0$$

$$n^2 - 11n - 4n + 44 = 0$$

$$n(n - 11) - 4(n - 11) = 0$$

$$(n - 11)(n - 4) = 0$$

So, $\qquad n = 11, 4$

So number of terms should be 4 or 11   **Ans.**

9 Draw a line segment AB of length 8 cm. Taking A as centre, draw a circle of   **3**
radius 4 cm and taking B as centre, draw another circle of radius 3 cm. Construct
tangents to each circle from the centre of the outer circle.

Solution:

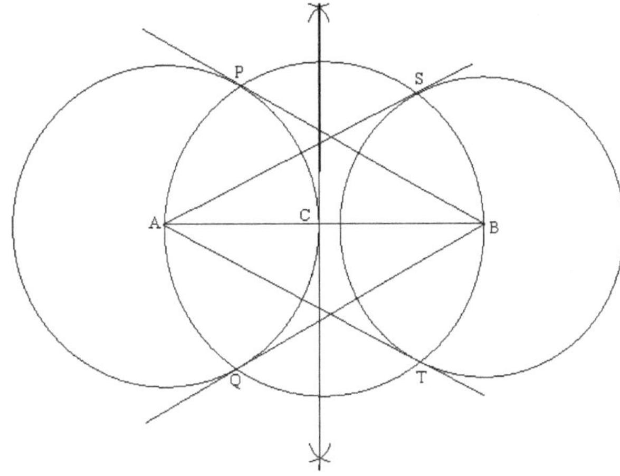

1. Draw a line segment AB = 8 cm
2. From a as centre, draw a circle of radius 4 cm and from B as centre draw
   another circle of 3 cm radius.
3. Draw perpendicular bisector of AB, which meets AB at C.
4. Take C as Centre and BC as radius draw a circle which centre smaller circle
   at S and T respectively and bigger circle at P and Q respectively.
5. Join AS and AT.
6. Join BP and BQ.
   These are the required tangents.

10 In a two digit number, the ten's digit is bigger. The product of the digits is 27 and   **3**
the difference between two digits is 6, find the number.

Solution:

Let unit digit is 'x' so ten's digit is $(x + 6)$, as given ten's digit is bigger.
So number is $= 10(x + 6) + x = 11x + 60$
According to question: $x (x + 6) = 27$
$$x^2 + 6x = 27$$
$$x^2 + 6x - 27 = 0$$
$$x^2 + 9x - 3x - 27 = 0$$
$$x(x + 9) - 3(x + 9) = 0$$
$$(x + 9)(x - 3) = 0$$
$$x = 3 \; or -9$$
but the number is positive so number $= 11 \times 3 + 60 = 93$ **Ans.**

Section C

11 The length of the shadow of a tower standing on level plane is found to be $2y$ **4**
metres longer when the sun's altitude is 30° than when it was 45°. Prove that the
height of the tower is $y(\sqrt{3} + 1)$ meters'.

Solution:

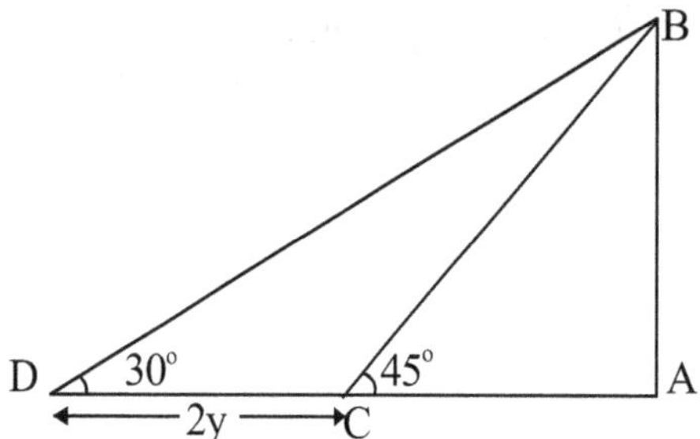

In the given figure AB is the tower and its shadow is AC when altitude is 45° it is 2y meter longer when altitude changes to 30°.

In triangle BAC tan BAC $= \dfrac{AB}{AC}$ ($\tan \theta = \dfrac{\text{perpendicular}}{\text{base}}$)

$1 = \dfrac{AB}{AC}$ => AB = AC   (i)

In triangle BAC, tan 30° $= \dfrac{AB}{AD}$

$$\dfrac{1}{\sqrt{3}} = \dfrac{AB}{AC + 2y}$$

$$\sqrt{3}AB = AB + 2y$$

$$\sqrt{3}AB - AB = 2y$$

$$AB(\sqrt{3} - 1) = 2y$$

$$AB = \dfrac{2y}{\sqrt{3} - 1} \times \dfrac{\sqrt{3} + 1}{\sqrt{3} + 1}$$

$$AB = \dfrac{2y(\sqrt{3} + 1)}{3 - 1} = \dfrac{2y(\sqrt{3} + 1)}{2}$$

$$AB = y(\sqrt{3} + 1)$$

12   If the mode of the following frequency distribution is 31, then find the value of p.   **4**

Class	5 – 15	15 – 25	25 – 35	35 – 45	45 – 55
Frequency	3	p	15	11	6

Solution:

Class	Frequency
5 - 15	3
15 - 25	p
25 - 35	15
35 - 45	11
45 - 55	6

Formula for mode $= l + \left(\dfrac{f_1 - f_0}{2f_1 - f_0 - f_2}\right) \times h$

Since mode is 31 so modal class for given distribution is $25 - 35$

Lower limit of modal class $(l) = 25$

Frequency of modal class $(f_1) = 15$

Frequency of class preceding the modal class $(f_0) = p$

Frequency of class succeeding the modal class $(f_2) = 11$

Class height $h = 10$

Substitute these values in the formula

$$31 = 25 + \left(\frac{15-p}{30-p-11}\right) \times 1031 - 25$$

$$= \left(\frac{15-p}{19-p}\right) \times 106$$

$$= \frac{150-10p}{19-p}\,114 - 6p$$

$$= 150 - 10p$$

$$4p = 36$$

$$p = 9 \qquad \textbf{Ans.}$$

13

Case Study based – 1 (Sanchi Stupa)

The Great Stupa at Sanchi is one of the oldest stone structures in India and an important monument of Indian Architecture. It was originally commissioned by the emperor Ashoka in the 3rd century BC. Its nucleus was a simple hemispherical brick structure built over the relics of the Buddha. It is a perfect example of a combination of solid figures. A big hemispherical dome with a cuboidal structure mounted on it. (Take $\pi = \frac{22}{7}$)

(a) Calculate the volume of the hemispherical dome if the height of the dome is 21 m.   1

     (i)   19404 m^3

     (ii)   20000 m^3

     (iii)   15000 m^3

     (iv)   19000 m^3

Solution:

Option (i) is correct

Height can be taken as radius of the tomb, so $r = 21$ m

Volume of hemisphere $= \dfrac{2}{3} \pi r^3$

$$= \dfrac{2}{3} \times \dfrac{22}{7} \times 21 \times 21 \times 21 = 19404 \text{ m}^3$$

(b) The formula to find the Volume of Sphere is-

    (i) $\dfrac{2}{3} \pi r^3$

    (ii) $\dfrac{4}{3} \pi r^3$

    (iii) $4 \pi r^3$

    (iv) $\dfrac{4}{3} \pi r^2$

Solution:

Option (iii) is correct

(c) The cloth require to cover the hemispherical dome if the radius of its base is 14m is

    (i)   1222 m^2
    (ii)   1232 m^2
    (iii)   1200 m^2
    (iv)   1400 m^2

Solution:

Option (ii) is correct

Radius $r = 14$ m

Cloth required to cover = its curved surface area $= 2\pi r^2$

$$= 2 \times \dfrac{22}{7} \times 14 \times 14 = 1232 \text{ m}^2$$

(d) The total surface area of the combined figure i.e. hemispherical dome with radius 14m and cuboidal shaped top with dimensions 8m × 6m × 4m is:

    (i)   1200 m^2
    (ii)   1232 m^2
    (iii)   1392 m^2
    (iv)   1932 m^2

Solution:

Option (iii) is correct

Total required area = CSA of dome + lateral surface area of cuboid + area of roof

$$= 1232 + (2(8{+}6) \times 4) + 8 \times 6$$
$$= 1392 \text{ m}^2$$

(e) The volume of the cuboidal shaped top is with dimensions mentioned in question 4:

    (i)   182.45 m^3
    (ii)   282.45 m^3
    (iii)   292 m^3
    (iv)   192 m^3

Solution:

Option (iv) is correct.

Volume of cuboidal shaped $= l \times b \times h$

$$= 8 \times 6 \times 4 = 192 \text{ m}^3$$

14

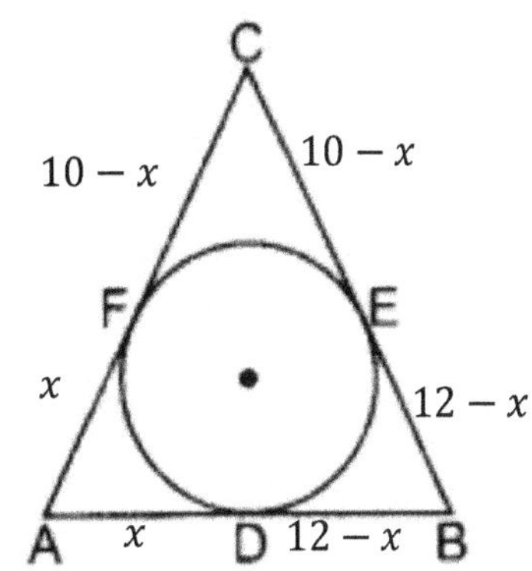

Varun has been selected by his School to design logo for Sports Day T-shirts for students and staff. The logo design is as given in the figure and he is working on the fonts and different colors according to the theme. In given figure, a circle with centre O is inscribed in a $\triangle ABC$, such that it touches the sides AB, BC and CA at points D, E, and F respectively. The lengths of sides AB, BC, and CA are 12 cm, 8 cm, and 10 cm respectively.

(a) Find the length of AD: 1
      (i)   7 cm
      (ii)   8 cm
      (iii)   5 cm
      (iv)   9 cm

Solution:
Option (i) is correct
AB = 12 cm, BC = 8 cm and CA = 10 cm
Let AD = AF = x cm   (tangents from external point are equal)

BD = BE = 12 − x cm, AD = AF = x cm and CF = CE = 10 − x cm
So BC = BE + CE
     8 = 12 − x + 10 − x
    2x = 22 − 8 = 14
     x = 7 cm   **Ans.**

(b) Find the length of BE: 1
      (i)   8 cm
      (ii)   5 cm
      (iii)   2 cm
      (iv)   9 cm

Solution:
Option (ii) is correct
BE = 12 − x = 12 − 7 = 5 cm

(c) Find the length of CF: 1
      (i)   9 cm
      (ii)   5 cm
      (iii)   2 cm
      (iv)   3 cm

Solution:
Option (iv) is correct
CF = 10 − x = 10 − 7 = 3 cm

(d) If radius of the circle is 4 cm, find the area of triangle AOB.   1

(i)   20 cm^2
(ii)   36 cm^2
(iii)   24 cm^2
(iv)   48 cm^2

Solution:

Base AB = 12 cm, drop perpendicular OP on AB i.e. radius = 4 cm

So area of triangle AOB $= \dfrac{1}{2} \times$ base $\times$ height

area of triangle AOB $= \dfrac{1}{2} \times 12 \times 4$

area of triangle AOB $= \dfrac{1}{2} \times 12 \times 4 = 24$ cm^2 **Ans.**

(e) Find the area of triangle ABC:

(i)   50 cm^2
(ii)   60 cm^2
(iii)   100 cm^2
(iv)   90 cm^2

Solution:

Option (ii) is correct

area of triangle ABC = area of $\triangle$ AOB + area of $\triangle$BOC + area of $\triangle$AOC

$$= 24 + \dfrac{1}{2} \times 8 \times 4 + \dfrac{1}{2} \times 10 \times 4$$
$$= 24 + 16 + 20 = 60 \text{ cm}^2 \qquad \textbf{Ans.}$$

Solved Model Test Paper – 3

Class – X : Session – 2021 – 22

(MATHEMATICS) – Term 2

Time Allowed: 2 hour   **Maximum Marks: 40**

General Instructions:

1. The question paper consists of 14 questions divided into 3 sections A, B, C.
2. All questions are compulsory.
3. Section A comprises of 6 questions of 2 marks each.
4. Section B comprises of 4questions of 3 marks each. No internal choice in this section.
5. Section C comprises of 4 questions of 4 marks each. It contains two case study based questions. Attempt any four questions from each case study.

Section A

Q. No.   **Marks**

1   Is 184 a term of the sequence 3,7,11........?   **2**

Solution:

Let 184 is the nth term of the sequence, where n is a natural number.

So an = 184

First term a = 3

Common difference d = 7 – 3 = 4

$a + (n - 1) d = 184$

$3 + (n - 1)4 = 184$

$3 + 4n - 4 = 184$

$4n = 185$

$n = \dfrac{185}{4}$, which is not a natural number,

so 184 is not a term of this sequence. **Ans.**

2   The weight of 45 children in a class were recorded, to the nearest kg, as follows   **2**

Wt. (in ncarest kg)	46	48	50	52	53	54	55
No. of children	7	5	8	12	10	2	1

Solution:

weight (in kg)	No. of children (f)	frequency
46	7	7
48	5	7+5=12
50	8	12+8=20
52	12	20+12=32
53	10	32+10=42
54	2	42+2=44
55	1	44+1=45
	n = 45	

(75)

Since n = 45 is odd therefore $median = \left(\frac{n+1}{2}\right)^{th}$ observation

$$= \left(\frac{45+1}{2}\right)^{th} = 23^{rd} \; observation$$

In cumulative frequency column value against 23 or more is 52, so median = 52

Ans.

3 Find the value(s) of m for which the equation $(m + 4)x^2 + (m + 1)x + 1 = 0$ has real and equal roots. **2**

Solution:

Compare it to $ax^2 + bx + c = 0, a \neq 0$

a = m + 4, b = m + 1, c = 1

since roots are equal, so discriminant $b^2 - 4ac = 0$

$(m + 1)^2 - 4\times (m+4) \times1=0$

$m^2 + 2m + 1 - 4m - 16 = 0$

$m^2 - 2m - 15 = 0$

$m^2 - 5m + 3m - 15 = 0$

m(m – 5) +3(m – 5) = 0

(m – 5) (m + 3) = 0

m = 5, –3 **Ans.**

4 If the mode of the following frequency distribution is 13, then find the value of p. **2**

Class	0 – 5	5 – 10	10 – 15	15 – 20	20 – 25	20 – 25
Frequency	2	P	18	10	8	5

Solution:

Mode for the following distribution $= l + \left(\frac{f_1-f_0}{2f_1-f_0-f_2}\right) \times h$

Since mode for the given distribution is 13, so modal class = 10 – 15

Frequency of modal class $(f_1) = 18$

Frequency of class preceding the modal class $(f_0) = $ p

Frequency of class succeeding the modal class $(f_2) = 10$

Lower limit of modal class $(l) = 10$

Class height $(h) = 5$

Substitute all these values in the above formula:

$$13 = 10 + \left(\frac{18 - p}{36 - p - 10}\right) \times 5$$

$$13 - 10 = \left(\frac{90 - 5p}{26 - p}\right)$$

$$3 = \left(\frac{90 - 5p}{26 - p}\right)$$

$$78 - 3p = 90 - 5p$$
$$2p = 12$$
$$p = 6 \qquad \textbf{Ans.}$$

5 The largest sphere is carved out of a cube of side 7 cm. Find the volume of sphere. **2**

Solution:

Side of cube = 7 cm, so radius of largest sphere carved out from this cube = 3.5 cm

$$\text{volume of sphere} = \frac{4}{3}\pi r^3$$

$$= \frac{4}{3} \times \frac{22}{7} \; 3.5 \times 3.5 \times 3.5$$

$$= \frac{4}{3} \times 22 \times 0.5 \times 3.5 \times 3.5$$

$$= \frac{539}{3} = 179.67 \text{ cm}^3 \qquad \textbf{Ans.}$$

6 Divide 216 into three parts which are in A.P. and the product of two smaller parts is 5040. **2**

Solution:

Let first term be 'a' and common difference be 'd' then three terms in A.P. = $a - d, a, a + d$

$$a - d + a + a + d = 216$$

$$3a = 216$$

$$a = 72$$

so terms are $72 - d, 72, 72 + d$

Now $(72 - d) \times 72 = 5040$

$$72 - d = \frac{5040}{72} = 70$$

$$-d = 70 - 72 => -2$$

$$d = 2$$

So three terms are $a - d, a, a + d = 72 - 2, 72, 72 + 2 = 70, 72, 74 \qquad \textbf{Ans.}$

Section B

7 In the figure given: from an external point P, tangents PA and PB are drawn to a circle. CE is a tangent to the circle at D. If AP = 15 cm, find the perimeter of the triangle PEC. **3**

Solution:

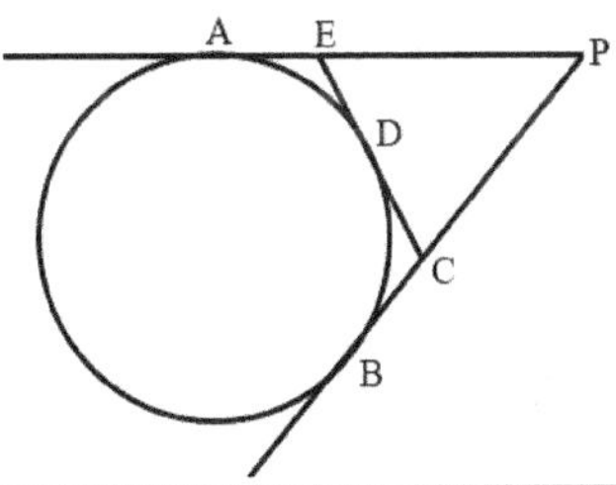

Tangent PA= 15 cm (given)

PA = PB   [Tangents from an external point to a circle are equal]

Perimeter of triangle PEC = PE + EC + PC

$$= PE + ED + CD + PC \qquad [EC = ED + CD]$$
$$= PE + EA + CB + PC \qquad [ED = EA \text{ and } CD = CB]$$
$$= PA + PB$$
$$= 15 + 15$$
$$= 30 \text{ cm} \qquad \textbf{Ans.}$$

8   In the figure, the sides AB, BC and CA of triangle ABC touch a circle with centre O and radius r at P, Q and R respectively. Prove that: **3**

Area $(\triangle ABC) = \dfrac{1}{2}$ (perimeter of $\triangle$ ABC)×r

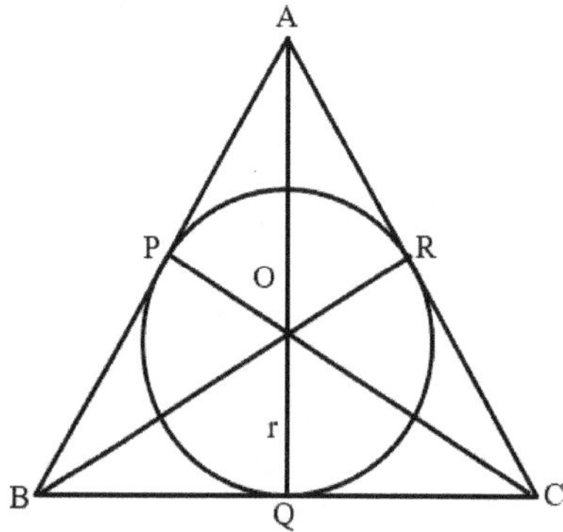

Solution:

Join $OP \perp AB$, $OR \perp AC$ and $OQ \perp BC$ [radius makes 90° with tangent at point of contact]

Area of triangle ABC = area of triangle BOC + area of triangle AOC + area of triangle AOB

area of triangle $\quad ABC = \dfrac{1}{2}BC \times r + \dfrac{1}{2}AC \times r + \dfrac{1}{2}AB \times r$

area of triangle $\quad ABC = \dfrac{1}{2}r(BC + AC + AB)$

area of triangle $\quad ABC = \dfrac{1}{2} \times$ perimeter of triangle ABC $\times$ r

                                                   Proved

9   Draw a line segment of length 6.5 cm and divide it in the ratio 3 : 4. Measure the two parts.   **3**

   Solution:

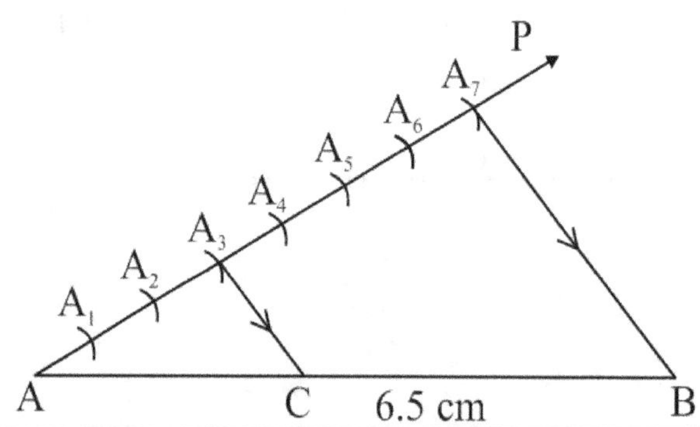

1. Draw a line segment AB = 6.5 cm.
2. Construct a raw with an acute angle and take a point P an it.
3. Make $A_1, A_2, A_3, \ldots\ldots, A_6, A_6$ an AP at equal intervals so that: $A\,A_1 = A_1A_2 = A_2A_3\ldots\ldots\ldots A_5A_6 = A_6A_7$.
4. Join A_7B.
5. Through A_3 draw a line parallel to A_7B, which meets AB at C.
   So, AC: CB = 3:4

10   The angle of elevation of a jet plane from a point A on the ground is 60°. After flight of 15 seconds, the angle of elevation changes to 30°. If the jet plane is flying at a constant height of 1500 m, find the speed of the jet plane.   **3**

Solution:

In the following figure a plane is flying at 1500 m and making angle of elevation at point D = 60°. After 15 seconds angle of elevation changes to 30°.

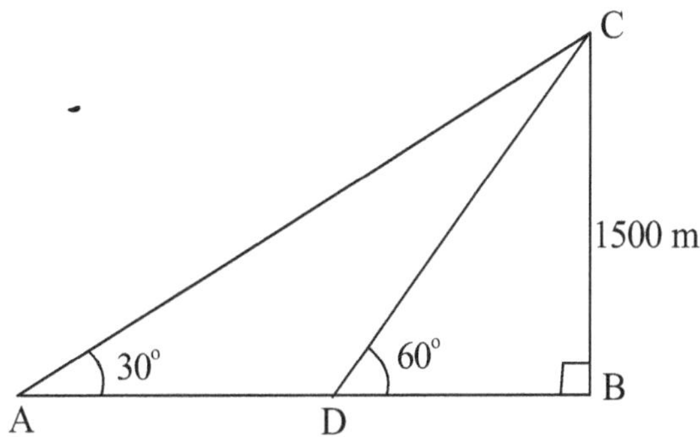

In triangle DBC, $tan\,60° = \dfrac{BC}{DB}$ $\left(tan\,\theta = \dfrac{perpendicular}{base}\right)$

$$\sqrt{3} = \frac{1500}{DB}$$

$$DB = \frac{1500}{\sqrt{3}} \times \frac{\sqrt{3}}{\sqrt{3}} = \frac{1500\sqrt{3}}{3} = 500\sqrt{3}$$

In triangle ABC, $tan\,30° = \dfrac{BC}{AB}$

$$\frac{1}{\sqrt{3}} = \frac{1500}{AB}$$

$$AB = 1500\sqrt{3}$$

So distance travelled in 15 seconds AD = AB − DB

$$= 1500\sqrt{3} - 500\sqrt{3} = 1000\sqrt{3} = 1000 \times 1.732 = 1732 \text{ m}$$

$$Speed = \frac{distance}{time}$$

$$speed = \frac{1732}{15}$$

$$Speed = 115.47 \text{ m/sec} \qquad \textbf{Ans.}$$

Section C

11   A container shaped like a right circular cylinder having diameter 12 cm and height 15 cm is full of ice cream. The ice cream is to be filled into cones of height 12 cm   **4**

and diameter 6 cm, having a hemispherical shape on the top. Find the number of such cones which can be filled with ice cream.

Solution:

Radius of cylindrical container 'r' = 6 cm and 'h' = 15 cm

Volume of ice cream in container $= \pi r^2 h = \pi \times 36 \times 15 = 540\pi \ cm^3$

Radius of cone and hemisphere 'r_1' = 3 cm and height of cone 'h_1' = 12 cm

Volume of ice cream contained in 1 cone = Volume of cone + volume of hemisphere

$$= \frac{1}{3}\pi r_1{}^2 h_1 + \frac{2}{3}\pi r_2{}^3$$

$$= \frac{1}{3}\pi \times 9 \times 12 + \frac{2}{3}\pi \times 27$$

$$= 36\pi + 18\pi = 54\pi \ cm^3$$

$$\text{number of cone} = \frac{\text{volume of container}}{\text{volume of ice cream in 1 cone}}$$

$$= \frac{540\pi}{54\pi} = 10 \text{ cones} \qquad \textbf{Ans.}$$

12 The marks obtained by 120 students in mathematics test is given in the following distribution. **4**

Marks	0 – 20	20 - 40	40 – 60	60 – 80	80 – 100	Total
No. of students	17	f_1	32	f_1	19	120

The mean of the following distribution is 50 and the sum of the frequencies is 120. Find the missing frequencies f_1 and f_2.

Solution:

Marks	No. of students (f)	Class mark (x)	fx
0 - 20	17	10	170
20 - 40	f_1	30	$30f_1$
40 - 60	32	50	1600
60 - 80	f_2	70	$70f_2$
80 - 90	19	90	1710
	$\Sigma f = 68 + f_1 + f_2$		$\Sigma fx = 3480 + 30f_1 + 70f_2$

$$mean = \frac{\Sigma fx}{\Sigma f}$$

$$50 = \frac{3480 + 30f_1 + 70f_2}{120}$$

$$3480 + 30f_1 + 70f_2 = 6000$$

$$30f_1 + 70f_2 = 2520$$

$$3f_1 + 7f_2 = 252 \qquad (i)$$

$$68 + f_1 + f_2 = 120$$

$$f_1 + f_2 = 52 \qquad (ii)$$

substitute $f_1 = 52 - f_2$ in equation (i) we get

$$3(52 - f_2) + 7f_2 = 252$$

$$156 - 3f_2 + 7f_2 = 252$$

$$4f_2 = 252 - 156$$
$$4f_2 = 96$$
$$f_2 = 24$$

substitute f_2 in equatin (ii) we get $f_1 + 24 = 52$

$$f_1 = 28$$

Ans. $f_1 = 28$, $f_2 = 24$

Case Study based – 1 (Heights and distances)

13

Priya was walking on the road when she saw a high tower in front of her. She observed that when she was standing at point A, the angle of elevation to the top of the tower was 30°. On moving 20 m towards the tower to point B, the angle of elevation changed to 45° as shown in the figure.

(a) What is the height of the tower?

    (i)   14.35 m   1

    (ii)   16.76 m

    (iii)   27.32 m

    (iv)   None of these

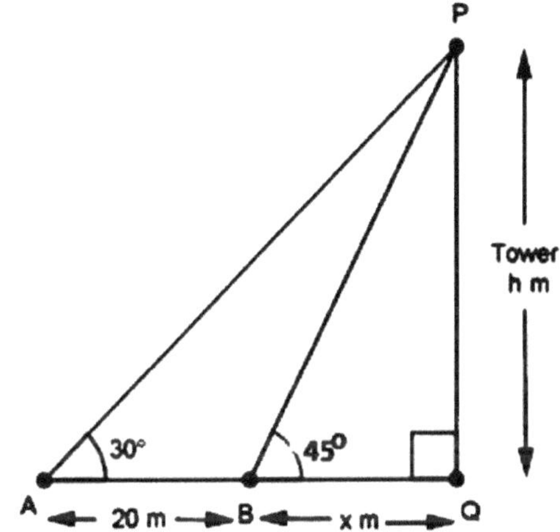

Solution:

Option (iii) is correct

In triangle BQP, $\tan 45° = \dfrac{h}{x}$ $\left(\tan \theta = \dfrac{perpendicular}{base}\right)$

$$1 = \frac{h}{x}, \text{ so } h = x$$

In triangle AQP, $\tan 30° = \dfrac{h}{x+20}$

$$\frac{1}{\sqrt{3}} = \frac{h}{h+20} \qquad \text{(as } h = x)$$

$$\sqrt{3}h = h + 20$$

$$\sqrt{3}h - h = 20$$

$$h(\sqrt{3} - 1) = 20$$

$$h = \frac{20}{\sqrt{3}-1} \times \frac{\sqrt{3}+1}{\sqrt{3}+1} = \frac{20(\sqrt{3}+1)}{2} = 10 \times 2.732 = 27.32m \ \textbf{Ans.}$$

(b) What is the distance of Priya when she is standing at point B from the base of the tower?   1

    (i)   14.35 m

(ii)   16.76 m

(iii)   27.32 m

(iv)   None of the above

Solution:

Option (iii) is correct

As $x = h$ so $x = 27.32$ m   **Ans.**

(c) What is the value of angle APQ?   1

    (i)   30°

    (ii)   60°

    (iii)   90°

    (iv)   120°

Solution:

Option (ii) is correct.

As triangle AQP is a right angled triangle, so angle APQ = 180 – (90 + 30) = 60°

Ans.

(d) What is the value of angle BPQ?   1

    (i)   30°

    (ii)   45°

    (iii)   90°

    (iv)   120°

Solution:

Option (ii) is correct

As triangle BQP is a right angled triangle, so angle BPQ = 180 – (90 + 45) = 45°

Ans.

(e) What was the distance of Priya from the base of the tower when she was standing at the point A?   1

    (i)   47.32 m

    (ii)   45.32 m

    (iii)   43.32 m

    (iv)   41.31 m

Solution:

Option (i) is correct

Since $x = 27.32$ so distance of point A from Q = 20 + 27.32 = 47.32   **Ans.**

Case Study based – 2 (Upstream and Downstream)

14

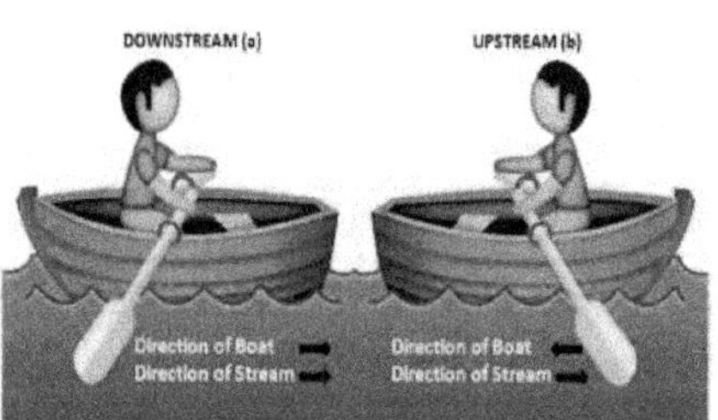

The speed of a motor boat is 20 km/hr. A boat goes 15 km upstream and return to the original point. For covering the distance of 15 km the boat took 1 hour extra for upstream than downstream.

(a) Let speed of the stream be x km/hr. then speed of the motorboat in upstream shall be:

    (i) $20 - x$ km/hr

    (ii) $x - 20$ km/hr

    (iii) $20 + x$ km/hr

    (iv) 20 km/hr

Solution:

Option (i) is correct

As in upstream boat has to go to the opposite to stream.

(b) What is the relationship between speed, distance and time?

    (i)   speed = distance × time

    (ii)   distance = speed / time

    (iii)   speed = time / distance

    (iv)   None of these

Solution:

Option (iv) is correct

(c) What is the right quadratic equation for the speed of the stream?

    (i) $x^2 + 30x - 200 = 0$

    (ii) $x^2 + 20x - 400 = 0$

    (iii) $x^2 + 30x - 400 = 0$

    (iv) $x^2 - 20x - 400 = 0$

Solution:

Option (iii) is correct

Upstream speed = $(20 - x)$ km/hr

Downstream speed = $(20 + x)$ km/hr

Time to go 15 km upstream = $\dfrac{15}{20-x}\, hr$ $\left(time = \dfrac{distance}{speed}\right)$

Time to go 15 km downstream = $\dfrac{15}{20+x}\, hr$

$$\frac{15}{20 - x} - \frac{15}{20 + x} = 1$$

$$\frac{300 + 15x - 300 + 15x}{(20 - x)(20 + x)} = 1$$

$$30x = 400 - x^2$$

$$x^2 + 30x - 400 = 0 \qquad \textbf{Ans.}$$

(d) What is the speed of the stream?

    (i)   20 km/hour

    (ii)   10 km/hour

    (iii)   15 km/hour

    (iv)   25 km/hour

Solution:

Option (ii) is correct

On solving equation obtained in (c) part

$$x^2 + 40x - 10x - 400 = 0$$

$$x(x + 40) - 10(x + 40) = 0$$

$$(x + 40)(x - 10) = 0$$

$x = -40, 10$, since speed can not be negative, so speed of stream = 10 km/hr.

(e) How much time boat took in downstream to cover the distance?

    (i)   90 minutes

    (ii)   15 minutes

(iii)   30 minutes

(iv)   45 minutes

Solution:

Downstream speed $= 20 + x$

$= 20 + 10 = 30$ km/hr

Time to go 15 km in downstream $= \dfrac{15}{30} = \dfrac{1}{2} hr = 30\ minutes$ **Ans.**

Unsolved
Question Papers

Model Test Paper – 1

Class – X : Session – 2021 – 22

(MATHEMATICS) – Term 2

Time Allowed: 2 hour   **Maximum Marks: 40**

General Instructions:
1. The question paper consists of 14 questions divided into 3 sections A, B, C.
2. All questions are compulsory.
3. Section A comprises of 6 questions of 2 marks each. Internal choice has been provided in one question.
4. Section B comprises of 4questions of 3 marks each. No internal choice in this section.
5. Section C comprises of 4 questions of 4 marks each. No internal choice is given. It contains two case study based questions. Attempt any four questions from each case study.

Section A

Q. No.   **Marks**

1 Which is the 37th term of the A.P.: $\sqrt{x}, 3\sqrt{x}\ 5\sqrt{x}, \ldots \ldots ?$ 2

2 If the discriminant of the equation $6x^2 - bx + 2 = 0$ is 1, then find the value of 'b'.   2

3 A ladder 15 m long just reaches the top of a vertical wall. If the ladder makes an angle of 60° with the wall, then what will be the height of the wall?   2

4 The first term of an A.P. is -7 and the common difference 5. Find its 18th term and the general term.   2

5 To circles with centers X and Y touch externally at P. If tangents AT and BT meet the common tangent at T, then prove that AT = BT.   2

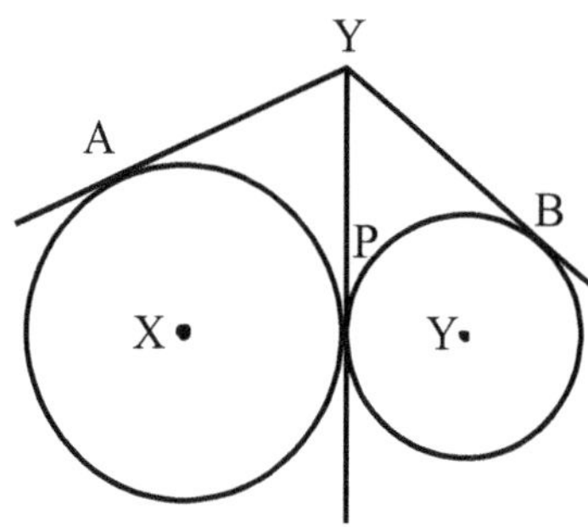

6 If the mode of the following frequency distribution is 31, then find the value of p.   2

Class	5 – 15	15 – 25	25 – 35	35 – 45	45 – 55
Frequency	3	P	15	11	6

Or

The mean of 5 observations $x, x + 2, x + 4, x + 6\ and\ x + 8$ is 11, then find the value of x.

Section B

| 7 | Draw a circle of radius 6 cm. From a point 10 cm away from its centre, construct the pair of tangents to the circle and measure their lengths. | 3 |

| 8 | A train travels a distance of 300 km at constant speed. If the speed of the train is increased by 5 km/hour, the journey would have taken two hours less. Find the original speed of train. | 3 |

| 9 | If the pth term of an A.P. is $\dfrac{1}{q}$ and the qth term is $\dfrac{1}{p}$, show that the sum of first pq terms is $\dfrac{(pq+1)}{2}$. | 3 |

| 10 | A kite flying at a height of 75 m from the level ground is attached to a straight string inclined at 60° to the horizontal ground. Find the length of the string to the nearest meter. | 3 |

Section C

| 11 | From the top of a cliff 90 m high, the angles of depression of the top and bottom of a tower are observed to be 30° and 60° respectively. Find the height of tower. | 4 |

| 12 | Write the median class of the following distribution: | 4 |

Class intervals	0 – 10	10 – 20	20 – 30	30 – 40	40 – 50	50 – 60	60 – 70
Frequency	4	4	8	10	12	8	4

13

Case Study based – 1 (Rubix Cube)

A teacher in his class brought a Rubix cube as shown in the figure. He wanted to explain surfaces and volumes of the Rubix cube. He explained that the Rubix cube is a combination of smaller cubes. It contains cubes in 3 × 3 × 3 manner. Each cube has 2 cm × 2 cm × 2 cm.

(a) What is the total surface area of the Rubix cube?

    (i)   216 cm²   **1**

    (ii)   108 cm²

    (iii)   132 cm²

    (iv)   5127.07 cm²

(b) What is the volume of the Rubix cube?   1

    (i) 127 cm^3

    (ii) 216 cm^3

    (iii) 324 cm^3

    (iv) 108 cm^3

(c) What is the total surface area of each individual cube?   1

    (i) 32 cm^2

    (ii) 28 cm^3

    (iii) 24 cm^3

    (iv) 48 cm^3

(d) What is the total surface area when four Rubix cube are joined in a row?   1

    (i) 1200 cm^2

    (ii) 648 cm^2

    (iii) 642 cm^2

    (iv) 600 cm^2

(e) What is the total surface area of the Rubix cube, when one small cube is removed   1
from corner?

    (i) 192 cm^2

    (ii) 216 cm^2

    (iii) 210 cm^2

    (iv) 132 cm^2

14

Case Study based – 2 (Ice Cream)

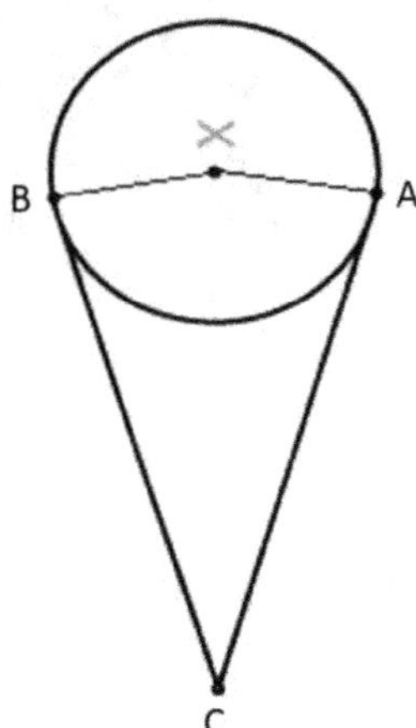

Chris was eating ice-cream on the way back home from shop. When he observed the shape of ice-cream, he found it as the circle with 2 tangents.

(a) What is the value of ∠CAX.   1

    (i) $80°$

    (ii) $90°$

    (iii)   95º

    (iv)   100º

(b) Which are the two tangents in the figure?   **1**

    (i)   AX and BX

    (ii)   AX and AC

    (iii)   BX and BC

    (iv)   AC and BC

(c) If $\angle AXB = 130º$ then find the $\angle ACB$.   **1**

    (i)   30º

    (ii)   50º

    (iii)   70º

    (iv)   None of these

(d) If AC = 45 cm and BC = $15x$, then find the value of x.   **1**

    (i)   2

    (ii)   4

    (iii)   3

    (iv)   1

(e) If AC = 45 cm and BC = $15x$, then find the length of the chord AB, where AB = $7x + 2$.   **1**

    (i)   22

    (ii)   24

    (iii)   23

    (iv)   21

Model Test Paper – 2

Class – X : Session – 2021 – 22

(MATHEMATICS) – Term 2

Time Allowed: 2 hour   **Maximum Marks: 40**

General Instructions:
1. The question paper consists of 14 questions divided into 3 sections A, B, C.
2. All questions are compulsory.
3. Section A comprises of 6 questions of 2 marks each. Internal choice has been provided in one question.
4. Section B comprises of 4 questions of 3 marks each. Internal choice has been provided in one question.
5. Section C comprises of 4 questions of 4 marks each. No internal choice is given. It contains two case study based questions. Attempt any four questions from each case study.

Section A

Q. No.   **Marks**

1   Find the curved surface area of a right circular cone of height 15 cm and base diameter   2
16 cm.

2   The arithmetic mean of the following distribution is 25. Determine the value of p.   2

Class	$0-10$	$10-20$	$20-30$	30 - 40	$40-50$
Frequency	5	18	15	p	6

3   In the given figure, AQ, AR and BC are tangents to a circle with centre O. If AB = 7   2
cm, BC = 5 cm and AC = 5 cm, then find the length of the tangent AQ.

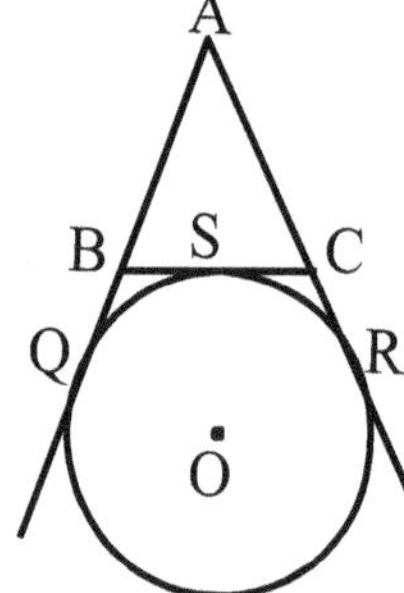

4   Find the value of k for which the roots of the following equations are real and equal: 2
$x^2 - 8kx + 2k = 0$

Or

Find the value(s) of p for which the quadratic equation $2x^2 + 3x + p = 0$ has no real
roots.

5   Determine 'a' so that $2a + 1$, $a^2 + a + 1$ and $3a^2 - 3a + 3$ are consecutive terms of an   2
A.P.

| 6 | If the median of the data $6, 7, x - 2, x, 17, 20$ written in ascending order, is 16. Then find the value of x. | 2 |

Section B

| 7 | From the top of a tower, a man finds that the angle of depression of a car on the ground is 30°. If the car is at a distance 40 m away from the tower, find the height of the tower in nearest meter. | 3 |

Or

If the altitude of the sun is at 30°, then the height of the vertical tower that will cast a shadow of length 30 m on the ground is:

| 8 | Draw a line segment AB = 7 cm. Taking A as centre, draw a circle of radius 3 cm. From point B, construct a pair of tangents to the circle with centre A. | 3 |

| 9 | If the angles of a triangle are in A.P. the greatest angle is twice the least. Find all angles of the triangle. | 3 |

| 10 | The product of Rahul's age five years ago with his age 9 years later is 15. Find Rahul's present age. | 3 |

Section C

| 11 | A person standing on the bank of a river observes that the angle of elevation of the top of a tree standing on the opposite bank is 60°. When he retreats 40m away from the bank, he finds that the angle of elevation to be 30°. Find: | 4 |

(i) The height of the tree

(ii) The width of the river, correct to two decimal places.

| 12 | In the given figure, two circles with centre A and B touch each other externally. PM = 15 cm is tangent to circle with centre A and QN = 13 cm is tangent to circle with centre B from external points P and Q. If PA = 17 cm and BQ = 12 cm, find the distance between the centers A and B of circles. | 4 |

Case Study based – 1 (Football)

Ritu packed a football as a gift for her brother's birthday in a cuboidal box whose diameter is same as that of length of base of the box having length, breadth and height respectively 23 cm, 23 cm and 28 cm.

(a) The volume of the football is:

1

    (i) 3581 cm^3

    (ii) 6373.19 cm^3

    (iii) 6451 cm^3

    (iv) 9807 cm^3

(b) Ritu covers the box with a wrapping sheet. The area of the wrapping sheet that covers the box exactly is:

1

    (i) 3634 cm^2

    (ii) 2533 cm^2

    (iii) 2584 cm^2

    (iv) 3813 cm^2

(c) The volume of the box is:

1

    (i) 25733 cm^3

    (ii) 18573 cm^3

    (iii) 14812 cm^3

    (iv) 77536 cm^3

(d) Half of the remaining volume of the box is filled with thermocol balls. Find the volume of the thermocol balls used.

1

    (i) 36150.9 cm^3

    (ii) 4219.405 cm^3

    (iii) 2764 cm^3

    (iv) 4048.05 cm^3

(e) The surface area of the football is:

1

    (i) 691.03 cm^3

(ii)   12772 cm^3

(iii)   15544 cm^3

(iv)   1662.57 cm^3

14   **Case Study based – 2 (Race)**

In a 100 m race a stop watch was used to find the time that it took a group of students to run 100 m.

(a) Estimate the mean time taken by a student to finish the race.   1

Time in seconds	0 – 20	20 - 40	40 – 60	60 - 80	80 - 100
Number of students	8	10	13	6	3

(i)   54

(ii)   63

(iii)   43

(iv)   50

(b) What will be the upper limit of the modal class?   1

(i)   20

(ii)   40

(iii)   60

(iv)   80

(c) The construction of cumulative frequency table is useful in determining the: 1

(i)   Mean

(ii)   Median

(iii)   Mode

(iv)   All of the above

(d) The sum of lower limit of median class and modal class is: 1

(i)   60

(ii)   100

(iii)   80

(iv)   140

(e) How many students finished the race within 1 minute?   1

    (i)   18

    (ii)   37

    (iii)   31

    (iv)   8

Class – X : Session – 2021 – 22

(MATHEMATICS) – Term 2

Time Allowed: 2 hour   **Maximum Marks: 40**

General Instructions:

1. The question paper consists of 14 questions divided into 3 sections A, B, C.

2. All questions are compulsory.

3. Section A comprises of 6 questions of 2 marks each. Internal choice has been provided in one question.

4. Section B comprises of 4 questions of 3 marks each. Internal choice has been provided in one question.

5. Section C comprises of 4 questions of 4 marks each. No internal choice is given. It contains two case study based questions. Attempt any four questions from each case study.

Section A

Q. No.		Marks
1	A kite is flying at a height of 75 m above the ground. The string attached to the kite is temporarily tied to the ground. If the inclination of the string with the ground is $60°$, then find the length of the string (in the nearest meter) assuming that there is no slack in the string.	2
2	If 35 is removed from the data: 30, 34, 35, 36, 37, 38, 39, 40, then the median increases by:	2
3	Find the length of tangent drawn to a circle with radius 5 cm from a point 13 cm away from the centre of the circle.	2
4	Find the number of cubes of side 2 cm which can be cut from a cube of side 6 cm.	2
5	A pole being broken by the wind, the top struck the ground at an angle of $30°$ and at a distance of 8 m from the foot of the pole. Find the whole height of the pole?	2
6	The mean of the following data is 16. Calculate the value of f.	2

Marks	5	10	15	20	25
No. of Students	3	7	f	9	6

Section B

7	A motor boat, whose speed is 9 km/hr. in still water, goes 12 km downstream and comes back in a total time of 3 hours. Find the speed of the stream.	3
8	Draw two tangents to a circle of radius 3.5 cm from a point P at a distance of 6.2 cm from its centre.	3
9	The angle of elevation of the top of a tower from two points P and Q at distances a and b respectively, from the base and in the same straight line with it, are complementary. Prove that the height of the tower is $\sqrt{ab}$.	3
10	Find the value of k for which the roots of the following equations are real and equal: $x^2 + 2 (k - 1) x + (k + 5) = 0$	3

Section C

11   A toy is in the form of a cone of radius 3.5 cm surmounted on a hemisphere of same radius. The total height of the toy is 5.6 cm. Find the total surface area of the toy. (Use $\pi = \frac{22}{7}$)   **4**

12   The following distribution shows the height of students of a certain class in a certain city: **4**

Height (in cm)	160 – 162	163 – 165	166 – 168	169 – 171	172 – 174
No. of students	15	118	142	127	18

Find the mean height of students.

13 **Case Study based – 1 (Circle)**

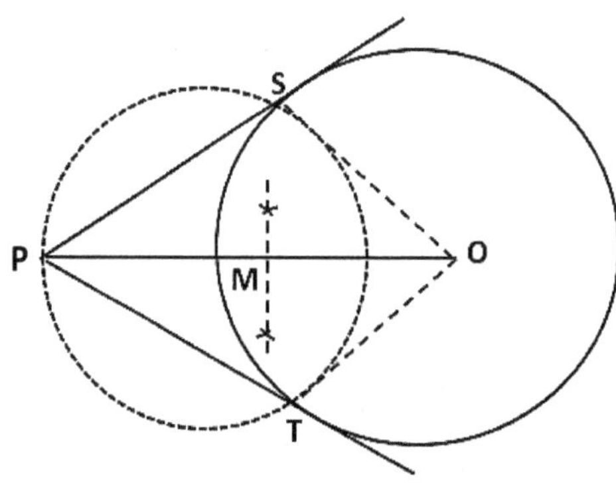

Madhuri has drawn a circle of radius 6 cm. From a point 10 cm away from its centre, she constructed the pair of tangents to the circle. Few questions came to her mind while drawing the tangents. Give answers to her questions by looking at the figure:

(a) What are the pair of tangents that are drawn?   **1**

     (i)   PS and PT

     (ii)   PO and PT

     (iii)   PS and PO

     (iv)   None of these

(b) What is the length of the tangents PS?   **1**

     (i)   6 cm

     (ii)   7 cm

     (iii)   8 cm

     (iv)   9 cm

(c) What is the length of the tangent PT?   **1**

     (i)   6 cm

     (ii)   7 cm

     (iii)   8 cm

     (iv)   9 cm

(d) What is the measurement of angle PSO?   **1**

(i)   30°

(ii)   60°

(iii)   180°

(iv)   90°

(e) Which theorem can be used to calculate the length of the tangent PS?   **1**

    (i)   Pythagoras theorem

    (ii)   Mid – point theorem

    (iii)   Gravity theorem

    (iv)   Euclid's lemma

14

Case Study based – 2

Aman got his name registered for a sprint race. The race is scheduled for a month later than the time he registered for the race. He started practicing for the race. His current run time is 51 sec for the distance to be covered in the race. He wants to reduce his time to 31 seconds. Answer the following questions

(a) What would be a suitable A.P. for the above situation?

    (i)   51, 53, 55 and so on.   **1**

    (ii)   51, 49, 47 and so on.

    (iii)   –51, –53, –55 and so on.

    (iv)   None of these.

(b) Would he be able to achieve his target in one month?

    (i)   Yes   **1**

    (ii)   No

(c) If Aman is able to achieve his target, then in how many days will he able to achieve it?   **1**

    (i)   10 days

    (ii)   11 days

    (iii)   12 days

    (iv)   13 days

(d) Which of the following is not a term of the A.P. found in part (a)?

    (i)   30

    (ii)   41

    (iii)   37

    (iv)   39

(e) If the nth term of an A.P. is given by $a_n = 2n + 3$, then what is the common difference of the A.P.?

    (i)   2

    (ii)   3

    (iii)   5

    (iv)   1

Class – X : Session – 2021 – 22

(MATHEMATICS) – Term 2

Time Allowed: 2 hour   **Maximum Marks: 40**

General Instructions:
1. The question paper consists of 14 questions divided into 3 sections A, B, C.
2. All questions are compulsory.
3. Section A comprises of 6 questions of 2 marks each. Internal choice has been provided in one question.
4. Section B comprises of 4questions of 3 marks each. Internal choice has been provided in one question.
5. Section C comprises of 4 questions of 4 marks each. No internal choice is given. It contains two case study based questions. Attempt any four questions from each case study.

Section A

Q. No.		Marks

1 The first term of an A.P. is -5, the last term is 45 and the sum of its terms is 120. Find the number of terms and the common difference of the A.P. **2**

2 For the following data, find mode: **2**

Class intervals	$1-3$	$3-5$	$5-7$	$7-9$	$9-11$
Frequency	14	16	4	4	2

3 Find the value of 'm', if the following equation has equal roots: **2**

$$(m-2)\,x^2 - (5+m)\,x + 16 = 0.$$

Or

If $ax^2 + bx + c = 0$ has equal roots, then find the value of 'c'.

4 In an AP, if m^{th} term is n and n^{th} term is m, show that its rth term is $(m + n - r)$. **2**

5 Twelve solid spheres of same size are made by melting a solid metallic cylinder of base diameter 2 cm and height 16 cm. The diameter of each sphere is: **2**

6 If the mean of 4, 5, a, 6, b, 9 and 11 is 10, then find the value of $(a + b)$. **2**

Section B

7 In the given figure, PQ is a chord of length 8 cm of a circle of radius 5 cm. The tangents at point P and Q intersect at point T. Find the length of tangent TP. **3**

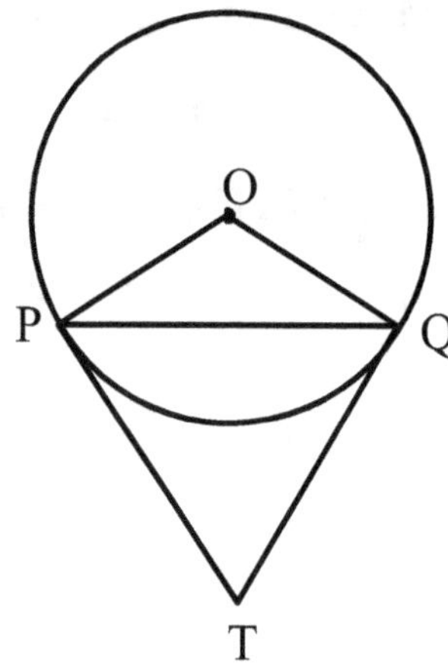

8   If two towers of height h_1 and h_2 subtend angles of 60° and 30° respectively at the midpoint of the line segment joining their feet, then find the value of $h_1 : h_2$.   **3**

Or

An observer 1.5 m tall is 28.5 m away from a tower 30 m high. The angle of elevation of the top of the tower from his eye is:

9   Construct two tangents PT and PQ to a circle of radius 4 cm and centre O such that $\angle TOQ = 120^{o}$.   **3**

10   If in the isosceles triangle ABC of figure given below, AB = AC, show that BF = FC.   **3**

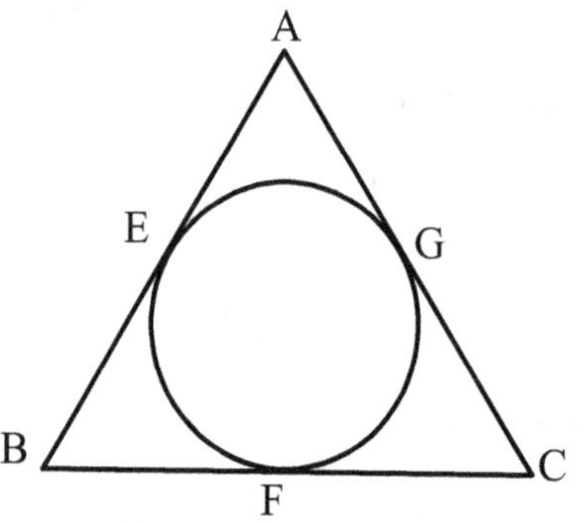

Section C

11   If the median of the following frequency distribution is 27.5, then find the missing frequencies.   **4**

Class intervals	$0-10$	$10-20$	$20-30$	$30-40$	$40-50$	$50-60$	Total
Frequency	3	f_1	20	15	f_2	5	60

12   A solid right circular copper cone of height 15 cm and radius 6 cm is melted, and smaller copper cones of height 3 cm and radius 2 cm are made. How many smaller cones can be made?   **4**

Case Study based – 1 (Eiffel Tower)

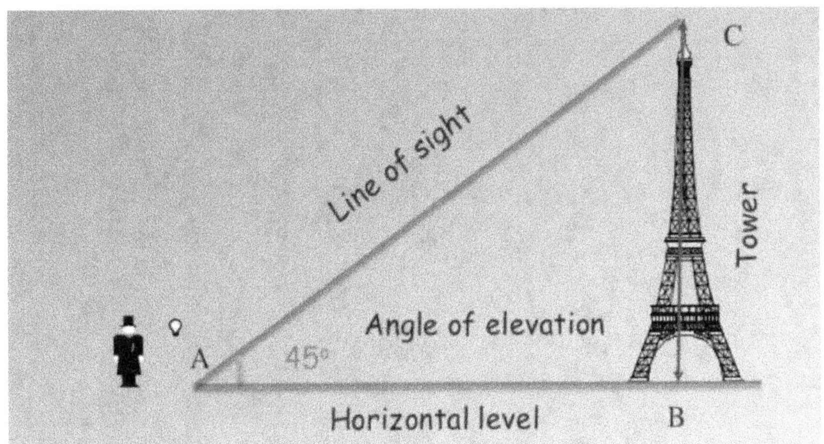

Mr. Henry visited the Eiffel tower. He was standing at a place from where the angle of elevation to the top of the tower was 45°. The height of the tower was 300m.

(a) At what distance was Mr. Henry standing from the tower?

    (i)   100 m

    (ii)   200 m

    (iii)   300 m

    (iv)   400 m

(b) What would be the angle of elevation of the mid – point of the tower as seen by Mr. Henry?

    (i)   26.56°

    (ii)   45°

    (iii)   22.5°

    (iv)   90°

(c) What is the length of the line of sight?

    (i) $100\sqrt{2}$ m

    (ii) $200\sqrt{2}$ m

    (iii) $300\sqrt{2}$ m

    (iv) $400\sqrt{2}$ m

(d) What is value of angle ACB?

    (i)   22.5°

    (ii)   45°

    (iii)   67.5°

    (iv)   90°

(e) Will the angle of elevation increase if Mr. Henry starts moving towards the tower?

    (i)   Yes

    (ii)   No

The angry Arjun carried some arrows for fighting with Bheeshm. With half the arrows, he cut down the arrows thrown by Bheeshm on him and with six other arrows, he killed the rath driver of Bheeshm. With one arrow each, he knocked down respectively the rath, flag and the bow of Bheeshm. Finally, with one more than four times the square root of total arrows, he laid Bheeshm unconscious on an arrow bed. Find the total number of arrows Arjun had. Answer the following questions, based on this information?

(a) What is the total number of arrows Arjun had?   **1**

    (i)   80

    (ii)   100

    (iii)   120

    (iv)   140

(b) What is the number of arrows used by Arjun to cut down the arrows thrown by Bheeshm?   **1**

    (i)   50

    (ii)   40

    (iii)   70

    (iv)   60

(c) What will be equation for the number of arrows left before killing Bheeshm (in terms of x)?   **1**

    (i) $\dfrac{x}{2} - 9$

    (ii) $\dfrac{x}{2} + 9$

    (iii) $\dfrac{2}{x} - 9$

    (iv) $\dfrac{x}{3} + 9$

(d) What is the number of arrows to kill Bheeshm?   1

    (i)   43

    (ii)   34

    (iii)   41

    (iv)   51

(e) According to the question, what will be the equation for the number of arrows used to kill Bheeshma (in terms of x)?   1

    (i) $1 + x\sqrt{4}$

    (ii) $1 + 4\sqrt{x}$

    (iii) $1 - x\sqrt{4}$

    (iv)   None of the above

Model Test Paper – 5

Class – X : Session – 2021 – 22

(MATHEMATICS) – Term 2

Time Allowed: 2 hour **Maximum Marks: 40**

General Instructions:
1. The question paper consists of 14 questions divided into 3 sections A, B, C.
2. All questions are compulsory.
3. Section A comprises of 6 questions of 2 marks each.
4. Section B comprises of 4 questions of 3 marks each. Internal choice has been provided in one question.
5. Section C comprises 4 questions of 4 marks each. No internal choice is given. It contains two case study based questions Attempt any four questions from each case study.

Section A

Q. No. **Marks**

1 Find the value of k for which the roots of the following equations are real and equal:
$(k - 12)\, x^2 + 2(k - 12)\, x + 2 = 0$ 2

2 Find the mean of the following distribution using: 2

Class	$0 - 10$	$10 - 20$	$20 - 30$	$30 - 40$	$40 - 50$
Frequency	12	16	6	7	9

3 The sum of the first n terms of an A.P. is $2n^2 + 5n$. Then find its nth term. 2

4 In the given figure, if angle OBC = 30°, then value of x is: 2

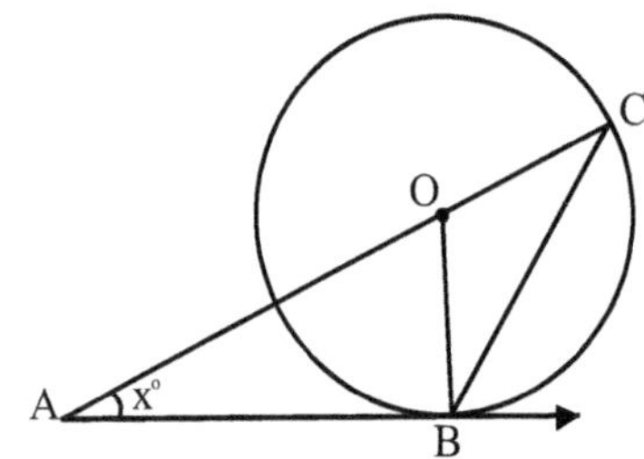

5 Two pipes are running together can fill a tank in $11\frac{1}{9}$ minutes. If one pipe takes 5 minutes more than the other to fill the tank, find the time in which each pipe would fill the tank. 2

6 The volume of a conical tent is 1232 m³ and the area of the bare floor is 154 m².
Calculate the: 2

(i) Radius of the floor.

(ii) Height of the tent.

(iii) Length of the canvas required to cover this conical tent if its width is 2 m.

Section B

| **7** | A tower is 64 m tall. A man standing erect at a distance of 36 m from the tower observes the angle of elevation of the top of the tower to be 60°. Find the height of the man. | **3** |

Or

In the given figure, ABCD is a rectangle with AD = 12 cm and DC = 20 cm, line segment DE is drawn making an angle of 30° with AD, intersecting AB in E. The length of DE is:

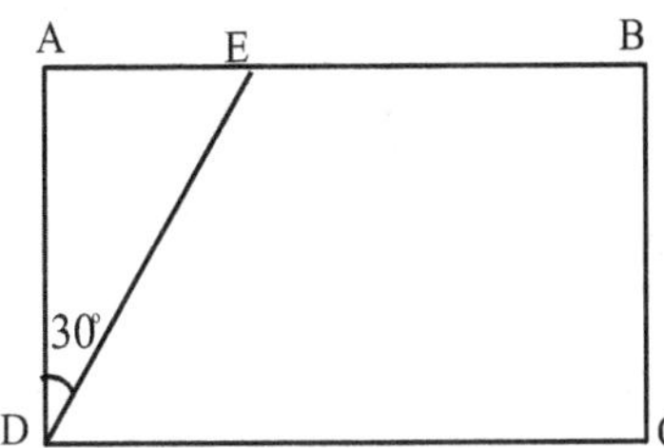

| **8** | Given below is a cumulative frequency distribution showing the marks secured by 50 students in a class. | **3** |

Marks	Below 20	Below 40	Below 60	Below 80	Below 100
Number of students	17	22	29	37	50

Find the median marks.

| **9** | Draw two circles of radii 3.5 cm and 5.5 cm which are 8 cm apart from their centre. Now from the centre of the bigger circle, construct a pair of tangents to the smaller circle. | **3** |

| **10** | A Mathematics aptitude test of 50 students was recorded as follows: | **3** |

Marks	50 - 60	60 - 70	70 - 80	80 - 90	90 - 100
No. of Students	4	8	14	19	5

Calculate Mode marks for the students.

Section C

| **11** | A wooden article as shown in the figure was made from a cylinder by scooping out a hemisphere from one end and a cone from other end. Find the total surface area of the article. | **4** |

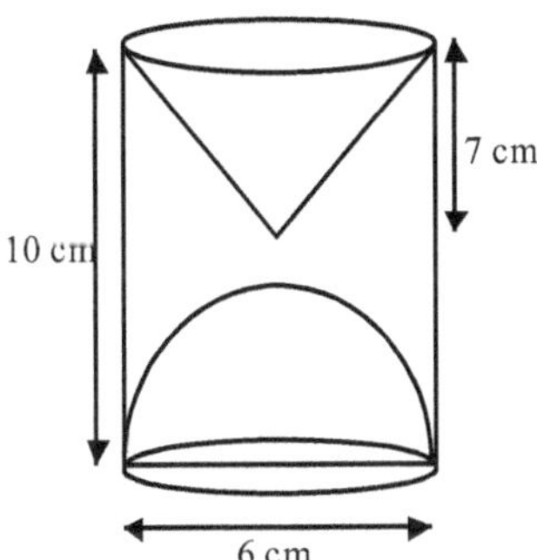

| **12** | A vertical tower stands on a horizontal plane and is surmounted by a vertical flagstaff of height h meter. At a point on the plane, the angle of elevation of the bottom of the flagstaff is α and that of the top of flagstaff is β Prove that the height of the tower is $$\frac{h \tan \alpha}{\tan \beta - \tan \alpha}.$$ | **4** |

13

Case Study based – 1 (Toffees and Candies)

Raj's mother gave him a packet of toffees and candies. The packet he had was having 120 toffees and candies. He started arranging toffees and candies in such a way that there were 3 in row 1, 5 in row 2, 7 in row 3 and so on. Answer the following questions using the above passage:

(a) What is the total number of rows formed by the number of candies he had?

    (i)   12

    (ii)   10

    (iii) 8

    (iv) 14

(b) How many candies are there in the last row?

    (i)   21

    (ii)   23

    (iii) 19

    (iv) 17

(c) How many candies would Raj require more, if he wishes to add two more rows to his pattern?

    (i)   46

    (ii)   48

    (iii) 50

    (iv) 44

(d) What is the difference of the candies between row 4th and row 8th?

    (i)   9

    (ii)   7

    (iii) 6

    (iv) 8

(e) If Raj eats 4 toffees, would it change the pattern he formed?

    (i)   Yes

    (ii)   No

14

Case Study based – 2

The above figure shows a circular field, which has road on all sides. Due to restriction the roads touch the circular field at one point.

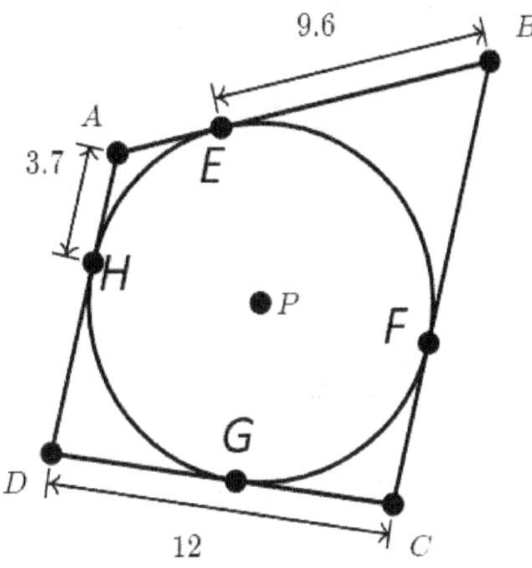

(a) How many tangents are there in the figure?   1
  (i)   1
  (ii)   2
  (iii) 3
  (iv)   4

(b) The tangents are drawn from an external point to a circle are: 1
  (i)   Equal
  (ii)   Perpendicular
  (iii) Unequal
  (iv)   None of the above

(c) In the figure EB = 9.6 cm, then what is the value of FB?   1
  (i)   3.7 cm
  (ii)   12 cm
  (iii) 9.6 cm
  (iv)   10 cm

(d) What is the perimeter of the road ABCD?   1
  (i)   50 cm
  (ii)   50.6 cm
  (iii) 60 cm
  (iv)   60.6 cm

(e) State true or false: The road ABCD is a quadrilateral drawn to circumscribe a   1
circle.
      Then AB + CD = AD + BC.
  (i)   True
  (ii)   False

Model Test Paper – 6

Class – X : Session – 2021 – 22

(MATHEMATICS) – Term 2

Time Allowed: 2 hour   **Maximum Marks: 40**

General Instructions:
1. The question paper consists of 14 questions divided into 3 sections A, B, C.
2. All questions are compulsory.
3. Section A comprises of 6 questions of 2 marks each. Internal choice has been provided in one question.
4. Section B comprises 4 questions of 3 marks each. No internal choice is given.
5. Section C comprises 4 questions of 4 marks each. No internal choice is given. It contains two case study based questions. Attempt any four questions from each case study.

Section A

Q. No.   **Marks**

1   Which term of the A.P. 3, 15, 27, 39, ... will be 132 more than its 54th term?   **2**

2   If the equation $(1 + m^2)\, n^2 x^2 + 2mncx + (c^2 - a^2) = 0$ has equal roots of x, prove that: $c^2 = a^2\,(1 + m^2)$.   **2**

Or

Perimeter of a rectangular plot is 180 m and its area is 1800 m^2. Find the length and breadth of the plot.

3   Prove that the angle between the two tangents to a circle drawn from an external point is supplementary to the angle subtended by the line segment joining the points of contact at the centre.   **2**

4   Divide 32 into four parts which are in A.P. such that the product of extremes is to the product of means is 7:15.   **2**

5   If the mode of the data 64, 60, 48, x, 43, 48, 43, 34 is 43, then find the value of $x + 3$.   **2**

6   A toy is in the form of a cone of radius 3.5 cm surmounted on a hemisphere of same radius. The total height of the toy is 5.6 cm. Find the total surface area of the toy. (Use $\pi = \frac{22}{7}$)   **2**

Section B

7   Find the value of p, if the mean of the following distribution is 20.   **3**

X	15	17	19	$20 + p$	23
F	2	3	4	$5p$	6

| 8 | If mode of the following distribution table is 53. Find the value of h (in nearest integer). | 3 |

class	20 - 30	30 - 40	40 - 50	50 - 60	60 - 70	70 – 80
Frequency	4	7	f	11	6	2

9   Draw two concentric circles of radii 3 cm and 6 cm. From a point on the outer circle, construct a pair of tangents to the inner circle. Measure their lengths.   **3**

10   A pole being broken by the wind, the top struck the ground at an angle of 30° and at a distance of 8 m from the foot of the pole. Find the whole height of the pole?   **3**

Section C

11   In figure given below, AB and CD are two common tangents of two circles with centers P and Q. These circles touch each other at M. If the common tangent at M meets AB and CD at X and Y respectively. Prove that $XY = \frac{1}{2}(AB + CD)$.   **4**

12   The radii of the base of two right circular solid cones of same height are r_1 and r_2 respectively. The cones are melted and recast into a solid sphere of radius R. Show that the height of each cone is given by $h = \dfrac{4R^3}{r_1{}^2 + r_2{}^2}$.   **4**

13   **Case Study based – 1 (Train)**

Two trains, train A and train B, departs from a station in 2 opposite directions Train A travels 360 km at a uniform speed. However, if the speed had been 5 km/h more, it would have taken 1 hour less for the same journey. On the other hand, train B covers a distance of 90 km at a uniform speed. But, if the speed had been 15 km/hr. more, it would have taken 30 minutes less for the journey. Based on this information, answer the following questions:

(a) Find the speed of train A: **1**
    (i)   44 km/hr.
    (ii)   40 km/hr.
    (iii)   30 km/hr.
    (iv)   34 km/hr.

(b) Find the speed of train B: **1**
    (i)   44 km/hr.
    (ii)   50 km/hr.
    (iii)   45 km/hr.
    (iv)   40 km/hr.

(c) If train A had covered 90 km instead of 360 km, then what would have been its speed (approximate)?   **1**
    (i)   10 km/hr.
    (ii)   32 km/hr.
    (iii)   24 km/hr.
    (iv)   19 km/hr.

(d) If train B had covered 360 km instead of 90 km, then what would have been its speed (approximate)?   **1**
    (i)   66 km/hr.
    (ii)   70 km/hr.
    (iii)   34 km/hr.
    (iv)   97 km/hr.

(e) According to the original condition, which train was faster?   **1**
    (i)   Train A
    (ii)   Train B

14   **Case Study based – 2 (Heights and distances)**

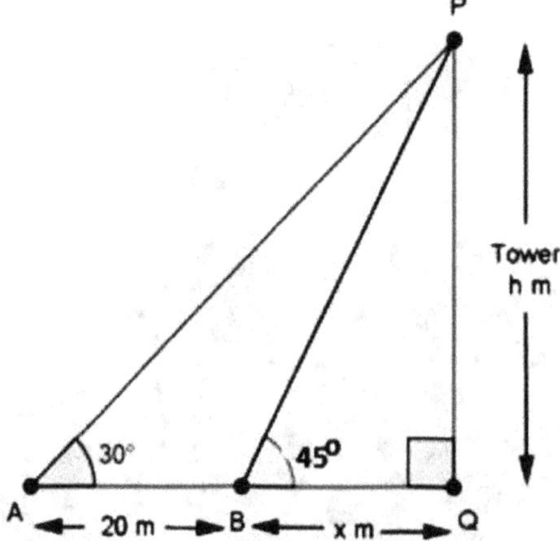

Priya was walking on the road when she saw a high tower in front of her. She observed that when she was standing at point A, the angle of elevation to the top of the tower was 30°. On moving 20 m towards the tower to point B, the angle of elevation changed to 45° as shown in the figure.

(a) What is the height of the tower?   1

    (i)   14.35 m

    (ii)   16.76 m

    (iii)   27.32 m

    (iv)   None of these

(b) What is the distance of Priya when she is standing at point B from the base of the tower?   1

    (i)   14.35 m

    (ii)   16.76 m

    (iii)   27.32 m

    (iv)   None of the above

(c) What is the value of angle APQ?   1

    (i) 30°

    (ii) 60°

    (iii) 90°

    (iv) 120°

(d) What is the value of angle BPQ?   1

    (i) 30°

    (ii) 45°

    (iii) 90°

    (iv) 120°

(a) What was the distance of Priya from the base of the tower when she was standing at point A?   1

    (i)   47.32 m

    (ii)   45.32 m

    (iii)   43.32 m

    (iv)   41.31 m

Model Test Paper – 7

Class – X : Session – 2021 – 22

(MATHEMATICS) – Term 2

Time Allowed: 2 hour　　　　　　　　　　　　　　　　　　　**Maximum Marks: 40**

General Instructions:
1. The question paper consists of 14 questions divided into 3 sections A, B, C.
2. All questions are compulsory.
3. Section A comprises of 6 questions of 2 marks each. Internal choice has been provided in three questions.
4. Section B comprises of 4questions of 3 marks each. Internal choice has been provided in one question.
5. Section C comprises 4 questions of 4 marks each. No internal choice is given. It contains two case study based questions. Attempt any 4 questions from each case study.

Section A

Q. No.　　　　　　　　　　　　　　　　　　　　　　　　　　　　**Marks**

1　　If the median of the data $6, 7, x - 2, x, 17, 20$ written in ascending order, is 16. Then　　2
find the value of x:

2　　A tower is 100 m high. Find the angle of elevation of its top from a point 100 m away　　2
from its foot.

Or

A tangent PA is drawn from an external point P to a circle of radius $3\sqrt{2}$ cm such that
the distance of the point P from O is 6 cm as shown in the figure. The value of $\angle APO$.

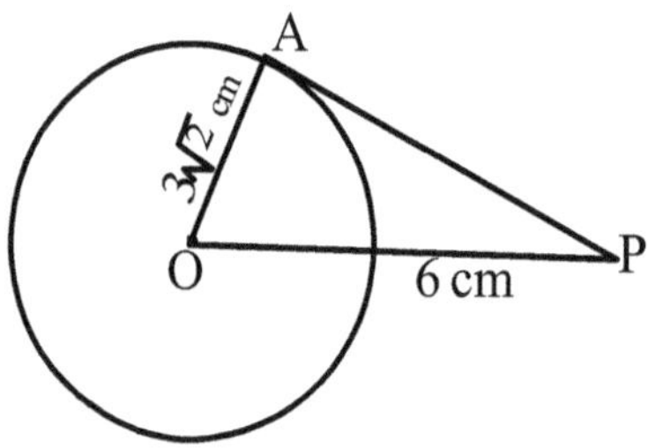

3　　In the given figure, $\angle ADC = 90^o$, BC = 38 cm, CD = 28 cm and BP = 25 cm. Find the　　2
radius of the circle.

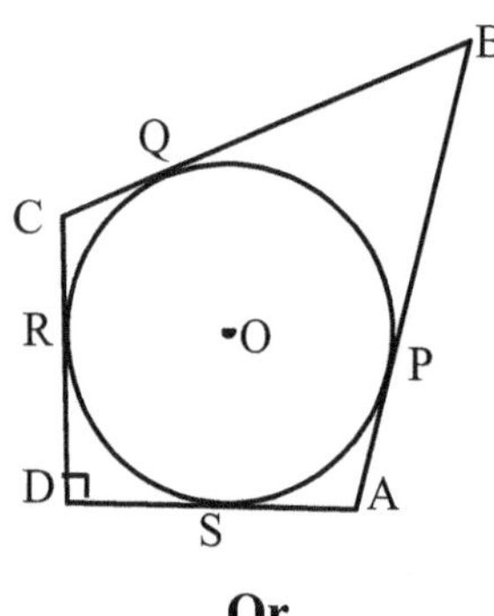

Or

In the given figure, AD = 8 cm, AC = 6 cm, and TB is the tangent at B to the circle with centre O. Find OT, if BT is 4 cm.

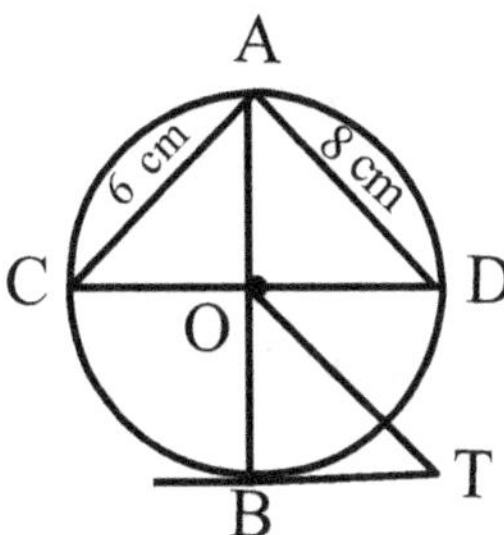

4 For the following data, find mode:

Class intervals	1 – 3	3 – 5	5 – 7	7 – 9	9 – 11
Frequency	14	16	4	4	2

2

5 A motorboat, whose speed is 15 km/hr in still water, goes 30 km downstream and comes back in a total of 4 hours 30 minutes. Find the speed of the stream.

2

6 Find the sum of all natural numbers from 1 to 100.

2

Or

Prove that the sum of first 'n' terms of the A.P: $\sqrt{2} + \sqrt{8} + \sqrt{18} +\ldots..$ is $\dfrac{n\,(n+1)}{\sqrt{2}}$.

Section B

7 Water running in a cylindrical pipe of inner diameter 7 cm is collected in a container at the rate of 192.5 liters per minute. Find the rate of flow of water in the pipe in km/h. (Use $\pi = \dfrac{22}{7}$).

3

8 A ladder rests against a vertical wall such that the top of the ladder reaches the top of the wall. The ladder is inclined at 60° with the ground, and the bottom of the ladder is 1.5 m away from the foot of the wall. Find: (i) The length of the ladder and (ii) The height of the wall.

3

9 Draw a line segment of length 7.6 cm and divide it in the ratio of 5: 8. Measure the two parts.

3

10 The given figure, shows the cross-section of a cone, a cylinder, and a hemisphere all with the same diameter 10 cm, and the other dimensions are as shown. Calculate:
(i) the total surface area
(ii) the total volume of the solid and
(iii) $d = \dfrac{m}{v}$

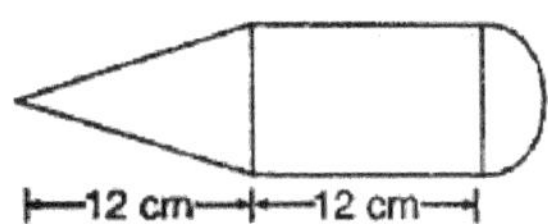

Section C

11 A circle is touching the side BC of triangle ABC at P and touching AB and AC produced at Q and R respectively. Prove that $AQ = \dfrac{1}{2} \times$ perimeter of triangle ABC.

4

12   The marks obtained by 120 students in mathematics test are given in the following distribution.   **4**

Marks	0 – 20	20 - 40	40 – 60	60 – 80	80 – 100	Total
No. of students	17	f_1	32	f_2	19	120

The mean of the following distribution is 50 and the sum of the frequencies is 120. Find the missing frequencies f_1 and f_2.

13   **Case Study based – 1 (Class Test)**

In a class test, the sum of Ranjana's marks in mathematics and English is 40. Had she got 3 marks more in mathematics and 6 marks less in English, the product of the marks would have been 360. On the other hand, Ranjana's friend, Maya scored 3 marks less in mathematics and 2 marks more in English than what Ranjana scored. Based on this information, answer the following questions:

(a) How much did Ranjana score in mathematics?

    (i)   12   **1**

    (ii)   21

    (iii)   26

    (iv)   Both (a) and (b)

(b) How much did Ranjana score in English?   **1**

    (i)   28

    (ii)   19

    (iii)   20

    (iv)   Both (a) and (b)

(c) How much did Maya score in Mathematics?   **1**

    (i)   9 or 18

    (ii)   15 or 24

   (iii) 23 or 29

   (iv) None of the above

(d) How much did Maya score in English?   **1**

   (i)   26 or 71

   (ii) 30 or 21

   (iii) 30 or 17

   (iv) 26 or 19

(e) Overall adding the marks of both the subjects, who scored more: Ranjana or Maya?   **1**

   (i)   Ranjana

   (ii) Maya

14   **Case Study based – 2 (T.V. Manufacturing company)**

During the summers of 2003, Manisha thought of starting some business of her own and lent some money from her father, and started a TV manufacturing company.Aftersome years, she was known as one of the leading manufacturers in her area and kept expanding her limit year by year. Assuming that the production increases uniformly year by year, the number of tv sets produced by her in the third year was 600 units and in the seventh year it was 700.

(a) What was the gradual increase in manufacture per year?

   (i)   20 units   **1**

   (ii) 25 units

   (iii) 30 units

   (iv) 45 units

(b) What was the production in first year?   **1**

   (i)   550 units

   (ii) 555 units

   (iii) 560 units

   (iv) 545 units

(c) What was the production in the tenth year?   1

    (i)   770 units

    (ii)   775 units

    (iii)   780 units

    (iv)   785 units

(d) What is the total production till seven years?   1

    (i)   4365 units

    (ii)   4370 units

    (iii)   4375 units

    (iv)   4380 units

(e) What is the difference between the production in fourth year and tenth year?   1

    (i)   150 units

    (ii)   180 units

    (iii)   170 units

    (iv)   185 units